Side Stream Re

Further meanderings of a chalk stream river keeper

RON HOLLOWAY

thinkology™

Published by Thinkology Ltd
www.thinkology.co.uk

Copyright © Ron Holloway, 2018

Cover design by Thinkology Ltd

ISBN: 978-1-5272-2112-3

It is my great privilege to bring Ron Holloway's manuscript to publication.
He was perhaps the wisest, best-informed and most insightful fisherman
I have ever had the pleasure to spend time with in or out of the water.
The text I present to you here is replete with good counsel on a great
many matters relevant to the preservation of our waterways and the fish
that inhabit them – and is the meanderings of a skilled and thoughtful
fisherman, which may just help you secure that catch of a lifetime.
I recommend it you.

I have enjoyed the pleasure of collating and publishing this book,
having forged a close friendship with Ron in his later years, rooted in a
shared love of fishing and – for both of us – in some painful personal
experiences through which we both relied very heavily on the love,
support and strength of those around us. When Ron's passing became
an imminent inevitability, we struck a pact: Ron would complete the
manuscript he had wrestled for years; I would bring it to publication.
Given my career as a car mechanic, salesman and property developer,
I remain deeply flattered that Ron believed I could keep my side of the
bargain.

I have been a fisherman for most of my adult life: a longstanding
member, and now chairman, of Errwood Fly Fishing Club in the Peak
District where I have fished for over forty years.

Much of what I know about fishing I was taught by my father-in-law,

Harry Hudson. Harry was a man with the perfect temperament for fishing: calm, patient and possessed of what often felt like a telepathic understanding of the trout and salmon he trailed. We spent countless days and nights together on the waterways of England, Ireland and Wales – though all too rarely Scotland.

I first encountered Ron Holloway in 2011 when I was invited by another great friend, Barry Hartle, to join the David Wallace fishing party to spend a springtime week fishing the Tweed. Such an invite is not one that any fisherman would wish to turn down. I leapt at the opportunity to fish one of the world's most celebrated rivers, piled a lifetime's preparation and a garage-full of paraphernalia into the back of the car for the long drive north, to St Boswells. The only thing cramping my excitement at the prospect was a hint of nervousness about whether all that I had learnt from Harry and others would equip me for the challenge of the Tweed. Like a nervous schoolboy on the first day of term, I worried that I might be branded as the one with 'all the gear, but no idea'.

Our home for the week would be a stone cottage high above the river, simple in construction, a true fisherman's facility – warm with conversation of the fishing in prospect. As David explained the custom and practice of the river to the newcomers amongst our group over a bottle – or more – of malt whiskey, I first heard the name Ron Holloway. The beat we fished was not served by a ghillie. Rather it was presided over by a legend of the sport who lived no further from the river than the cottage that would be our base for the week. We would never be far from Ron's watchful eye, we were warned; we should maintain high standards of etiquette and respect for the waterway or risk a stern word – and the prospect that our invite for future visits could be put at risk.

As I stood chest-high in the river the following morning I met Ron for the first time. Such was the billing he had been afforded in discussion the night before, I did not expect that he would arrive in and emerge from a bright yellow, battered hatchback. Nor was I prepared for a work of quite remarkable facial hair. The handlebars of Ron's moustache rested on long white curls of hair organised as gills along the jawline. There began a conversation which I hope to conclude with the publication of this book.

Over the years that followed, Ron and I enjoyed a great many conversations about the art of fishing, the maintenance of our waterways – and, over time, more personal and profound matters. That first visit had inspired many more. Ron's cottage quickly became my first resting place on arrival in St Boswells at the beginning of each cherished week on the river. There I had the pleasure to meet his wife, Paula. A wonderful woman who had willingly allowed Ron's love of the water to guide the big decisions of their life. When she passed away we drew Ron still-closer into our band. He would join us for dinner and a bottle or more of malt in the evening – over which discussion would range freely from tales of the day's catches and clangers to our experience of life and the changing world around us.

That tendency to more profound discussion grew as our journey through life rippled and surged like so many of the waterways we loved. Paula's death was a huge blow to Ron, it left him alone in the cottage they loved, more reliant than before on his friends – both local and amongst the many fishing parties that would pass through the estate each year.

I leant on Ron more than I ever had as a fisherman when, in the summer of 2015, after months of tests and tribulations, I was told that I had bowel and liver cancer such that I should start to measure my life in weeks and months at best. Nothing has ever given me greater cause for reflection than the prospect of dying before I was done living. Ron and I spoke many times on the phone in the days and weeks that followed my diagnosis – itself a matter of weeks after Paula had passed. From those conversations I recall the wisdom and grace of a man on whose opinion I had come to value, both in and out of the water.

I was incredibly fortunate that six weeks after I was diagnosed I was diagnosed again: this time as a reasonably healthy man who would live to fish another day. Whilst they were horrific beyond words to endure at the time, I have come to be grateful for that dark period and what it taught me – about life, about myself, and about my relationships with those around me. Great friendships emerge from such experiences deeper and stronger.

Six months later we lost Harry Hudson. As peacefully as he lived, he passed at home; his heart faded to nothing after years-long treatment for heart failure. He was ninety when he passed – survived by his wife Betty, loved beyond words by his son-in-law, his daughter Pat, and our son Matthew. His was a life lived. One that we can celebrate knowing that he saw and enjoyed more in his lifetime than he could ever have imagined growing up in the grounds of the 'big house' on the Annalee River in Cavan, Ireland.

Though it came too late in his life, Harry did join one of our trips to the Tweed. Too frail to fish for more than half an hour at a time, I am grateful that I was able to share with him one of my greatest pleasures – including, of course, the opportunity to meet Ron. I will forever be grateful that two men so important to me were able to meet, however briefly.

When Ron and I struck our pact, I hoped that he would have longer to work on his book. I was not ready to lose another great friend and mentor so soon. We spoke more and more over the last months of his life. It mattered to him that he should properly capture a lifetime of experience and expertise for others to enjoy and benefit from; that he would not complete the extended text he had originally set his sights on - 'the formation of chalk streams from the ice age to present day' – became obvious as his time with us ran short.

It was Ron's fitting wish that any proceeds from the sale of the book should go to the Wild Trout Trust: an organisation close to Ron's heart, and which he was instrumental in the formation and early success of. I am grateful to Matthew and his own mentor, Simon Milton, for helping me to fulfil my promise to publish.

As Ron said to me when he emailed me the final manuscript: 'Happy reading, best, Ron'.

THE WILD TROUT TRUST

Founded in 1995, the Wild Trout Trust is a conservation charity with a mission to improve the environment for wild trout across the UK and Ireland. We work with land owners, clubs and communities to support practical action that will improve the habitat for wild trout. Our members and supporters are typically fisherman – though we are not a fishing organisation.

We have in common with our members, supporters and partners, a passion for wild trout and the rivers they inhabit. The presence of wild trout in a given river is surely an indicator of the wider wellbeing of the river and its surroundings; we have a deep interest in the maintenance of a sustainable environment within which trout and other wildlife can sustainably coexist.

The Trust is led by a small group of committed trustees and a small, geographically dispersed staffing body, including a band of conservation officers around the country who provide that direct engagement with partners and projects which advance the cause of wild trout. Beyond that employed team, the Trust continues to rely on willing contributions from a band of volunteers who maintain our web presence and support our fundraising and events as well as a raft of other activities which maintain the Trust's momentum.

Ron Holloway was an inspirational founding father of the Trust. The Trust itself was founded by Charles Rangeley-Wilson and Richard Slocock – both experts in the field and highly skilled fishermen. Even before the Trust was formed, Ron was a leading thinker and practitioner of fishing and wild trout fishery management. His early engagement with and membership of the Trust – including but by no means limited to his membership of our earliest executive committees – was fundamental to the development and furtherance of our mission.

The Trust attracts funding from a range of different sources, including, most commonly, membership and donor contributions from relevant grant-making trusts, sponsorships and rod licence revenues for the many rivers on which we work. That fundraising effort is of course as challenging as it is important to the continued existence and effectiveness of the Trust. In 2017, we generated around £700,000 of income which enabled us to deliver almost 200 advisory visits and 80 practical projects in support of our mission.

Our support to partners and projects is rooted in a combination of relevant scientific research and our own practical experience. We also access the expertise and advice of an extended 'knowledge network' which includes academic researchers in relevant fields along with seasoned practitioners. Ron was an esteemed member of the early manifestations of that group. I remember taking many student groups to hear him speak passionately and insightfully about catchment management and habitat bottlenecks – topics now firmly established in mainstream thinking which at the time represented radical new discourse.

As we look to the future, the need for focused interest in wild trout and the environment they inhabit is as great or greater than ever. Whilst the Trust does not itself directly lobby national governments on relevant policy issues, we do support partner organisations who work with governments to help shape their thinking on areas of real concern to us, including issues such as land management, water abstraction and commercial sea trout netting in the North Sea.

We are delighted that David Hamnett has made it his mission to publish Ron's second manuscript, following Ron's passing in November 2016. David was a close friend of Ron in his later years on the Tweed. It is fitting that someone with David's passion and imagination has brought together this book.

We are of course thrilled that any surpluses generated from the sale of the book will accrue to the Trust – and we will ensure that they are invested in projects which make things better for wild trout and fulfil the memory of a wonderful man: Ron Holloway.

A PERSONAL MEMORY OF RON FROM CHARLES RANGELEY-WILSON

Ron and I drifted apart in the end. I was very sorry about this, but he had moved to Scotland and I had moved to Norfolk and, somehow, we never met again. I would have loved to have shown him some of the river projects we've completed in Norfolk lately, coming full circle to the first conversations we had about his work and Simon Cain's and Ron's philosophy of holistic catchment restoration.

It all started when I was teaching art at a school in Dorset, not quite sure if I had found the right career. I was getting into river conservation and had started some river projects with the school-kids. I had tried journalism too, was already a trout-nut and for some reason I had got into my head the idea of becoming a sort of writer / river-keeper. Tom Williams was my role model: he wrote wonderful stories about rivers, river-keeping and the countryside.

I had already met Simon Cain. I'd read about his work at Ballington on the Wylye in a book on chalk-streams: a book that also featured Ron and his river-narrowing projects on the Itchen. I remember that famous picture of Ron standing in a river, leaning on a scythe. His craggy face under a sloping tweed hat, that imposing beard and moustache. Ron even looked like a chalk landscape.

Simon knew Ron. I'm not sure if he introduced us. But I read an article by Ron on holistic catchment management. It made a lot of sense to me and I dared a letter to him. To my delight, Ron called me one Sunday to invite me over to the beat he kept at Martyr Worthy on the Itchen. I distinctly remember walking down the lane and through the little gate that lead to a path which threaded its way through willows and springs. I'd never seen a river quite like it: this majestic ooze of silky water, fractured by stands of starwort and *Ranunculus*, its surface peppered by armadas of olives and brown trout rising everywhere.

This was the first of many visits. They'd almost always involve the Chestnut Horse pub, a bacon sandwich and several pints of beer. Ron drank beer like he had hollow legs. The friendly formality of the mornings morphed into a much more passionate to-ing and fro-ing of ideas. Usually to-ing. There wasn't much fro-ing from me after a while. Even this was really only the first stirrings of the seismograph. One afternoon on my third or fourth visit we were walking along the river on the way back from the pub when I asked something mildly stupid about a particularly deep section of the river. I think I asked whether Ron planned to fill it with gravel. That was when Mt. Holloway first erupted. Of course, he wasn't going to fill it with gravel. What did I mean? Trout need deep water too. Did I not know that by now? Etc. etc. I must have looked mildly crestfallen, because the lava stream eased off after a minute or two, after which we carried on as if all was normal. It was. Ron was passionate. I understood that.

As the months and years passed, I became more and more absorbed by the idea of trying to consolidate this fractured movement of river restoration. I spoke to Ron about Trout Unlimited. Richard Slocock even wrote to TU to ask about founding an English chapter. But in the end, we plumped for a British version: the Wild Trout Society. Ron was in there from the beginning, along with me, Richard and Ronnie Butler, Roger Mills and Mike Weaver. Our earliest meetings might have been in Simon Cain's barn (though we moved to Dorset after a while) and, if so, that must have been when Simon dubbed us the Powder Keg Society. Who knows what inspired him? Ron, the gunpowder trail of beer, the difficult birthing pains of what would one day become the Wild Trout Trust? We all knew when it was time to buy Ron a pint. And when it was time not to buy him any more!

And look what the Wild Trout Trust has become now! Ron was in many ways its John the Baptist. He was a bit 'wild man of the wilderness', but we all loved him for it. More pertinently, Ron had taken river-keeping and put a progressive edge on it. He had pioneered all that work and he had written a large part of its gospel. What we learnt from Ron and what inspired the formation of the movement was: get on with it, think big. The River Itchen at Martyr Worthy is his lasting testament, carved into the English landscape.

INTRODUCTION

Since retiring from my work on the River Itchen, I have relocated to the Tweed Valley in the beautiful Scottish Borders and now live beside another wonderful river, the Tweed. The idea for this little book came about quite recently, during the consumption of a few pints of real ale at the bar of the Buccleuch Hotel in St Boswells in the Scottish Borders, after a fishless day on the lower beat of the Mertoun Estate on Tweed, in the company of three fishermen friends from Gloucestershire. As is the way with many fishermen who enjoy downing the odd jar of post-fishing ale, the conversation at the bar invariably turns very rapidly to storytelling about the day's fishing and tales of past or recent fishing escapades. Stories of the big one that came and missed the fly and the big one that came off at the net constantly fill the air; the story of the fish that the drunken ghillie knocked off the hook while trying to net it out before the fish had been played out is retold, and the stories of big fish hooked and played for hours and still lost are endless. Isn't it amazing how it is only the biggest fish that get away?! It is that huge fish that straightened out the hook that intrigues me... nobody will ever consider it may have been a duff hook to start with and the fish that straightened the hook was only a lively five-pound grilse. Even then, for long after, all those 'big' fish that have been lost seem to grow in size with every retelling of the story of how and when it got away.

Experience has taught me that these conversations between fishermen are far from uncommon in almost every fishing hotel bar in Scotland, let alone the rest of the world. There are invariably far more fish caught and lost at the bar in the evening after fishing than on the river during the day. Does this mean all fishermen are liars then? No, they are not generally in my experience – most are jolly good chaps – but one thing I have learnt in my professional fishing life is that there are some anglers who do suffer from that human frailty of exaggerating a wee bit. If the truth be known, we all as fishermen have been economical with the true facts at some time in our fishing lives, have we not? Come on now, think about it!

My fishing friends from Gloucestershire, knowing that I had recently published a book called *You Should Have Been Here Last Thursday*, asked if I was intending to write another book, as they all had so enjoyed reading my first book. My immediate answer was to say no, as I thought one book was enough; however, after a few more pints passed over the bar, they finally persuaded me to think again about writing a further book. I somewhat reluctantly agreed to consider their idea; however, I gave them one proviso: that they must come up with a suitable title. This decision by me was firmly influenced by this time by the amount of alcohol I had consumed!

The following morning, when I met the fishermen as they all gingerly stepped down from their vehicles at the fishing hut, all refused to admit that they were nursing a hangover. A strong brew of coffee in the fishing hut soon revived them and before they went off to fish they said they had unanimously agreed, after due discussion over breakfast at the hotel, that they had come up with a suitable title for my next book – their suggested title being 'Of Rods, Guns, Dogs and Fun'. Their rational reasoning being that as I had spent most of my professional working life with fishing rods and fishermen, shotguns and shooters, and working and training English springer spaniels, I should have some stories, thoughts and experiences worthy of recall.

I submitted rather reluctantly at the time and agreed to write another book. As I progressed with writing the first draft of this book, so my enthusiasm grew, and I increasingly became less enchanted with the suggested title. I therefore decided to change it to *Side Stream Reflections* for no other reason than *Side Stream Reflections* is a shorter title and reflects more accurately the diverse content of the book!

This little book is a compilation of some of my personal philosophies, experiences, and thoughts – both serious and light-hearted – about angling in general and my fishing, shooting and working spaniel experiences, all of which are based on true facts and experiences, although one or two stories may be cushioned with a modicum of poetic licence.

CHAPTER 1

PEOPLE WATCHING

In these modern times there are few sporting people who do not travel a great deal by air these days to and from their sporting destination, who have not at some time or other spent many a frustrating hour or two in the departure or arrivals lounge of some airport, either in the UK or somewhere else in the world, waiting for a delayed flight or connecting flight. I must admit that I do not mind this waiting too much these days since now that I have discovered a new hobby. I now use this wasted time in airport lounges people watching and reading other people's body language and trying to figure out in my mind if they are fishermen or shooters. I think most of us humans people watch, if not consciously then often subconsciously. It not only passes the time, but has, for me, become quite a fascinating occupation to while away the waiting time.

Glasgow, Edinburgh, Aberdeen and Inverness in the UK are great airports for fishermen spotting, either arriving or departing. The departure lounge at Heathrow for all flights heading to Scotland, Russia, Iceland or Alaska is also a good area for spotting salmon fishers and grouse shooters heading for the grouse moors, depending on the seasonable time of year when sporting people have a strong inherent desire to migrate north, either to grass a spring salmon or bag a brace or two of red grouse on the 'Glorious 12th' or stalk and down a twelve pointer red stag or even – if they are lucky – bag a McNab! A McNab is being successful at bagging at least one of all three species of the above game on the same day.

Recently, while waiting to meet a friend from the Southampton flight at Edinburgh, I had a few minutes to spare as the flight was running late, so I wandered into the café area and ordered a cup of cappuccino. Having spotted a free table, I sat down and started to people watch. On the adjoining table there was a city-suited gent with a closed laptop case and a copy of the FT neatly folded on top. The gentleman was deeply engrossed in the current month's copy of the *Trout & Salmon* magazine and I could not help observing which article he was reading so intently. It was Paul Procter's excellent recent article on fishing the blue-winged olive. Now, I asked myself, who was this man and where was he going. Dressed as he was, with laptop and FT at hand, he certainly had not been and was not going fishing this day. My guess was he was returning south after a business trip. He moved off to the departure area when his flight to London was called – so, yes, he came from the South of England and my guess was that he was a dry fly fisherman who lived in or near to London. Furthermore, he was a one-day-a-fortnight fisherman on a beat of the Middle Test in Hampshire. He had the mark of a typical 'Middle Test Man' as river keepers of the Test call these one-day-a-fortnight fly fisher!

Then there was the man on another table who wore a baseball cap, quality clean jeans, expensive trainers and a corduroy jacket over a quality check shirt, and he was also taking the London flight. His reading material was a carp magazine which caters for the dedicated specimen carp angler. He would be home within a couple of hours if he lived in London, but I was quite sure he would not be fishing for big carp in any of the Oxford lakes until later the following week. Why? Because he was married and had not been home for some time – observed gold wedding ring on wedding finger gave me that clue. My guess was that he was in the oil business and worked on an oil rig somewhere in the North Sea. He was tanned and fit and worked with his hands, as they were big and strong. Although casually dressed, the quality of his attire was expensive, so he obviously earnt good money.

A couple of years ago, when corporate entertainment was at its peak, I happened to be at Edinburgh Airport awaiting an incoming flight one Saturday evening, when, from a distance, I could not help but hear a loud military-type voice issuing commands to his troops, as the motley crew hove into view. This group, I quickly gathered, happened to be a group of city gents who were obviously going back to London after a six-day corporate jolly on the Junction Pool at Kelso on the Tweed. The party host could have come from nowhere else but straight off the playing fields of one of the top public schools, as his rather loud but cultured tones directed operations to his obviously wilting clients. The corporate host was all smiles and bonhomie, but his clients looked rather glum and bedraggled. Their body language screamed out to me that every man jack of them had but one wish... to get home! No doubt they had not caught many salmon, if any, and all were obviously suffering from an endless six-day hangover to boot and all for no charge! I am willing to bet none of them had ever held a two-handed salmon rod in their hands in their lives before they arrived on the water first thing on the previous Monday morning. That being the case, I bet the Junction Pool boatmen had a great week wet nursing six uninterested beginners!

Nevertheless, corporate entertainment does bring good money into the economy of the area, but the downside is usually they add little to maintain or improve the catch records of the beat who rely on good catch records to market their fishing on the same weeks in the seasons to come.

It is only the true salmon angler who really understands that even if you are fortunate enough or able to rent and pay up front for the best and most prolific beat on the river at the right time of year, that at times the party could well arrive on the Monday morning and not even take their rods out of the car because the river was either too low or in flood for the whole week. We have all been there and done that I am sure! That is salmon fishing the world over.

While the Junction Pool at Kelso is on my mind, that reminds me of a story that I heard recounted in a Kelso pub by one of the renowned boatman of the Junction Pool who happened to have Chris Tarrant, the host of ITV's *Who Wants to be a Millionaire?*, as his rod for the day. Now Chris is an experienced angler and knows the score when fishing; however, this day he was out in a boat with a boatman. Chris was fishing a heavy tube fly over the river as the boatman worked hard on the Junction Pool to hold the boat along the seam of water where the river Teviot and Tweed join. The Tweed was flowing well, as was the Teviot, which made it hard for the boatman to hold position. The conditions were made even worse as there was also a very strong cross-river wind blowing which made position-holding of the boat even more difficult for the boatman. Halfway down the drift and now mid-stream where the river is much wider, Mr Tarrant turned his head to the now sweating boatman and over his shoulder casually asked what he should do if he hooked a salmon. The boatman, without missing a stroke with his oars – knowing full well Mr Tarrant had his mobile switched on – came back in a flash with a deadpan face with the answer: "If you don't know then phone a bl***y friend."

On hearing that response Mr Tarrant fell off his seat and almost out of the boat, he laughed so violently. I think the ale flowed very well in the bar of the Ednam House Hotel that evening over the countless retelling of this incident.

CHAPTER 2

A PERFECT DAY'S
DRY FLY FISHING ON THE ITCHEN?

Having spent most of my working life as a river keeper on the Itchen in Hampshire, it is not surprising that one or two of my fishing stories and recollections emanate from those wonderful chalk stream rivers of that part of the world.

Back in the middle seventies, during that memorable hot summer of 1976 I think it was, I had been invited to fish the beat below my beat at Martyr Worthy, by the river keeper of the water below Easton Road Bridge which marked our bottom boundary. The keeper of that water was then and still is today a great friend of mine, Pat Fox.

Being an avid cricket player myself and a dedicated follower of any Test match that involved England, I remember the West Indies were touring the UK that summer... Sobers, Hall and Griffiths and co! What a side the 'Windies' had then.

That August day dawned with a cloudless blue sky and the promise of it being another scorching hot day. *Not the best of conditions for a day's dry fly fishing on the upper Itchen in August,* I thought, as I made my way down to the fishing hut at the lower end of the fishing. Nevertheless, I was grateful for the opportunity to fish such great water and to have it all to myself for the whole day. I was in dry fly paradise. Before leaving home, I had packed my fishing bag with a flask of coffee and a bottle of water and my wife had sliced up a whole tin of corned beef to make a pile of mustard-laden doorstep-thick sandwiches for my lunch. Knowing that a Test match was being played between England and the West Indies, I also put into my bag my little portable radio so I could keep tuning into TMS (Test Match Special) and listen to the rich dulcet Hampshire tones of John Arlott and the more cultured voice of Brian Johnson - both of whom would be commentating on the day's cricket action at Trent Bridge with inter over summaries by Trevor Bailey.

By the time the sun had attained its midday zenith, I had already made a quick armed reconnaissance with my rod at the ready, up the left-hand bank of the beat from bottom to top. Having completed this initial recce, I sat down in the shade of a willow tree for a cooling drink and a cigarette and just watched the river. I had covered several good wild trout along the way who were mainly taking the odd blue-winged olive as they hatched. Needless to say, I did not manage to land one or even get an offer. *Not bad for a start on a day such as this,* I thought to myself. On the way up the river, I had spotted one particularly good wild trout of, I guess, about 2 pounds in weight, which was sporadically rising tight under the far bank under some overhanging vegetation. I gave him a few chucks, but he diligently ignored me as the drag was horrendous from where I was crouched, as was the angle and position from which I had to cast even to cover him, so I soon moved on. However, I accurately marked his lie for future reference later in the day... *Maybe early evening with sedge as the light faded,* I thought to myself. I could, of course, have walked a couple of hundred yards downstream to cross over to the other bank via the footbridge and approach this trout from below his lie. But no, I decided that if he was to be mine I would do it the hard way and take him from my side of the river. Besides, the bank side vegetation was very thick on the far side of the river.

It was now early afternoon and the temperature had to be almost 90 degrees and not a trout was to be seen anywhere, let alone rising and taking insects off the surface. As it was so bright and hot there was little insect activity to be seen on or over the river surface at all, apart from the odd dragonfly darting about. Any fly fisher with a modicum of sense would, in these conditions, pack up and either go home, go to the pub, or gracefully retire to sit in the shade outside the fishing hut and snooze away the afternoon with a glass or two of river-chilled white wine in perfect peace and patiently wait for the evening rise. This was not for me this day as I had forgotten to bring the wine! I was determined to fish on through the heat of the afternoon, although I must admit it would not be with a great deal of confidence. I crept up the river, keeping well away from the river's edge so as not to scare any trout that were daft enough to show themselves in these conditions, but nothing took my attention until I rounded a bend in the river and approached the good fish that I had marked earlier in the morning. I found a good firm tussock of sedge that was conveniently growing on the river's edge, upon which I sat down to watch and wait. The trout's lie was fortunately in the shade of the tall bank side vegetation that grew his side of the river. The trout's lie was in the shade at this spot as owing to the bend in the river the sun was shining from a different angle. This fish, I am sure, had chosen this particular spot as his feeding lie in these bright sunlit conditions and with the water being really gin clear, for that very reason.

I patiently sat and watched and, lo and behold, after a few minutes my trout gently rose and sipped something off the surface. What he took I shall never know, but he rose periodically thereafter. By this time I had unpacked my corned beef sandwiches, which were rather soggy by now with the heat inside my fishing bag, and set them out to cool beside me in the shade of the tussock. Out came my flask and I poured a cup of coffee which I also set down beside me on the tussock and I slid off the tussock and sat crossed legged on the ground, leaning back against the tussock and watched my trout rise about once every three minutes, I reckoned. Out came my radio and I tuned it into TMS for the latest score in the Test match and wedged the radio into the sedge tussock so I could listen to the commentary with the sound turned right down as I fished. I was almost ready for the battle to commence but not completely, as I had not set out my dry fly box beside me on the tussock so I could readily change my choice of ammunition at will. This I did and dressed my first choice of fly that I had tied onto my light 7x tippet. With the sun in my eyes even with my cap pulled down and sunglasses on, I was unable to identify what insect or insects the trout was taking so gently. So I tied on a size 18 Lunn's Particular which is a spent pattern of the medium olive. With the bright sun direct into my eyes and the sun's reflection coming off the water, natural spent flies in such conditions are not always easy to spot or identify on a chalk stream, especially when the water is flowing quite quickly as it was opposite me or there is any surface disturbance created by submerged weed growths or other such like subsurface objects that break up the water's surface calm. Classic natural spent olives rest very flat on the surface film or, at times, they even lie within the surface film which makes them very difficult to identify, let alone see, from the river bank at the best of times.

From whatever position I tried, the drag over this trout was horrific, so I got little response from that trout whatever pattern I offered him. By late afternoon I had tried every pattern in my box and, damn it, I still could not get an offer or even put him down, which was the most frustrating part of it all. This trout was making a fool of me. I tried every known casting tactic to mitigate the drag problem during that sweltering afternoon between taking the odd sip of lukewarm coffee and a mouthful of corned beef sandwich between casts. All this accompanied by the Test match commentary. The only tactic that attracted the trout's attention was when I tied on a very small roof covered sedge fly I had tied the night before and cast the fly into the vegetation just upstream of his lie and then tweaked the fly out of the vegetation onto the water which, if it landed properly with a little slack in the tippet, gave me a few seconds of drag-free drift over the trout before the tippet straightened out and started to drag the fly, leaving a wake like a speed boat. Twice the trout poked his nose at my offering when I used that tactic successfully, but I rapidly ran out of sedge flies because, using such a fine tippet, I had left most of them in the bankside vegetation on the far side of the river. He just would not open his mouth wide enough!

As for the cricket during this monumental battle on the river, Sobers and Halford had put on almost two hundred runs between lunch and tea, and John Arlott waxed lyrical in his inimitable way over the excellence of Sobers' batting. By seven in the evening, or was it at close of play, I ran up the white flag and retired, hurt from my personal Test match with this trout. After packing up all my gear, through simulated gritted teeth and in a gentlemanly manner, I doffed my cap to my worthy adversary still lurking unharmed under the far bank. I slowly trudged up the river bank and headed home for supper. On the way, I walked over several good feeding trout who by this time had come out to play and were rising well. I am sure it would have been quite simple to catch one or two to break my duck, but I declined the temptation.

Later that evening, I met up with Pat Fox in the Chestnut Horse and bought him a couple of pints as a thank you for a most enjoyable day on his river. I regaled Pat with the story of my day and, just to rub salt into the wound, he said he knew that particular trout very well, as did all his fishermen who fished the beat, and they all had had similar battles with this trout. That alone made feel a little better.

A few weeks later Pat told me that the fish had finally been caught by one of his fisherman, who had very sneakily prepared his Test match ground the day before he fished by cutting down the tall bankside vegetation that hung over the trout's lie. This enabled him to present a dry fly without drag from a casting position directly downstream on the trout's side of the river. I cried, "No ball, umpire!"

Pat agreed entirely with my sentiments and bought me another pint.

For me that day's fishing was certainly one of the most memorable and enjoyable days dry fly fishing I had had for many a year and, even today, forty years on, that day still remains so vivid in my memory and always will. It was a blank day as to trout caught but who cares, that is what dry fly fishing is all about in my book. It was a great battle fought between me and one trout in beautiful surroundings on a grand day and I lost! Blank day maybe, but for me it was the most perfect day on a wonderful chalk stream... just Perfect!

Camping on a fish, as I did that day, is not uncommon practice on the chalk streams, especially when there is no other fisherman on the water. Some of today's serious fly fishing experts who write in magazines, and seem to catch trout every time they go fishing, will ask why did I not fish a nymph to that trout; a PTN or a small gold head would have probably done the trick or would have had a better chance to fool that fish. That may have been the case and a nymph or gold head may have killed that trout but, although I am not a dry fly snob and I do use nymphs and emerges when circumstances demand their use, that day, for me, was just not one of those circumstances. No, I wanted to catch that trout on a dry fly – that was the challenge I set myself. It was the ultimate challenge of the battle ground and the beautiful surroundings I enjoyed and all the attendant circumstances that made, for me, one of my most memorable days dry fly fishing. The only downside to cloud the memory of that great day was that England eventually lost the Test match.

CHAPTER 3

THE MOST EXPENSIVE FIVE MINUTES FISHING EVER?

There is an annual auction of fishing and fishing tackle and fishing memorabilia held each year at the Plaza Hotel in New York in aid of the Atlantic Salmon Federation. One of my rods, who visited USA regularly and attended these charity dinners each year, asked if he could offer a couple of days' fishing on the Martyr Worthy beat of the Itchen. This request was granted and when the auction was held the two days' fishing at Martyr Worthy fetched a huge amount of money – around $5000 to be more precise.

Finally, the charity days arrived after receiving several phone calls from a guy in New York who had successfully bid for the fishing, who needed directions etc., and said he would turn up at my cottage about 10am on the first day.

This he duly did, arriving in a taxi straight from Heathrow having just landed via Concorde from New York. After paying off the taxi driver from a huge wad of twenty-pound notes, I took his fishing bag and rod tube and we headed for the river. The excitement of just looking at the river from the footbridge sent this gentleman off into raptures of delight. His excitement was overpowering to say the least. He would stop and gulp "ooh" and "ah" at every trout he saw as he walked down the river. I could not keep him away from the river bank; I said that he would be walking down the river bank along which he would be fishing up within a few minutes, but it did not deter him one bit.

I assembled his rod and set up the leader and tippet and tied on a small sedge for starters, as I had little idea what standard of dry fisher this man was. He was like a jack-in-the-box, as he could not keep still and could not keep his eyes off the water and the rising trout. He asked me if we could walk the water again as he wanted to look at the trout and the river weed. When I had assembled his rod I suggested he should start fishing, but he said no, as he wanted to see more of the river first. So reluctantly I agreed to show him the whole river. He would not take his rod, he just wanted to walk the river. So off we went. He continually bombarded me with questions, all of which would be interspersed with mutterings like "What a privilege to be here", "What a wonderful river", "Fantastic", "Awesome", "Incredible". Midday came and passed, and he had not lifted his rod; he was still marvelling over the river. I suggested we walked over to the pub for a pint and a sandwich, but this he declined. By this time I was losing my patience a little as he had come all this way and had not fished at all so far. I made my excuse to go up to my cottage for my lunch and just to have a break, thinking that my absence just may encourage him to go and fish on his own, because I thought that he may not have the confidence to cast a rod in my company.

I arrived back around two o'clock and noticed that his rod had not been used and the guy had disappeared. I walked down to the lower river and found him stood in the middle of the footbridge staring into the deep pool above the bridge that always held some big trout. He was transfixed to the spot, as he could not take his eyes off these trout. I eventually dragged him away to the hut where his fishing rod awaited him. The time by now was well past three in the afternoon and still he had not made one cast to any of the rising trout. He said it was hardly worthwhile fishing now as his taxi was scheduled to pick him up at about three thirty, as he had to be at Heathrow to catch the four o'clock Concorde back to New York! I did manage to get him to cast a fly to one or two trout for about five minutes before we had to pack up and go up to meet his taxi.

On the way up to the car park he apologised profusely and said that he was unable to make it the following day as he had to fly off to Chicago the next morning from New York. He said he had had a super day and thanked me for looking after him and for answering all his questions.

This day visitor from New York paid $5000 for the fishing at a charity auction and heaven knows what a return ticket New York to London on Concorde had cost him. I know that chalk stream fishing can be expensive, but to me that was ridiculous and must be the most expensive five minutes dry fly fishing I have ever come across! $4000 to $5000 per minute?!

CHAPTER 4

GOOD LATERAL THINKING BY A HIGH COURT JUDGE

A high court judge once lived in my village who owned a couple of hundred yards of one bank of the main River Itchen that happened to run through his property. He was a very keen and competent dry fly fisherman.

Whenever he crossed my palm with silver, I would agree to cut the weed in his river and if there was sufficient silver to cover my palm, I would also trim his river side path so he could walk and fish along his side of the river. This arrangement went on for several years until the old boy died.

During his later years his eyesight was failing quite quickly, but he still fished right up to the end. To enable himself to fish without changing his fly, as he had great difficulty in tying on a fly with his poor eyesight especially when fishing late evening, I discovered that he had devised a great method of overcoming his incapacity.

I happened to be passing his house one evening when the judge appeared at his gate dressed for the river and clutching a handful of identical fly rods with identical reels and 9-foot 5x Platil leaders attached, all made up ready to fish. There were six rods in his hand, so I had to ask his honour what he intended to do with six fly rods... "Fish the bloody river, what else do you think I could do with them?" was his curt reply, as he headed towards the river. I dropped in step beside him and we conversed about fly life and what had been caught lately – and all those things that fly fishermen talk about – as we headed towards the river. By this time I had noticed that three of the rods had a Lunn's Particular attached and the other three rods had a good-sized sedge fly attached.

On reaching the river, I made to go back through the village and the judge made off down the river bank to the bottom part of his little piece of river. I doubled back when the judge was out of sight and crept down the other side of the river and stopped under a thick willow bush to watch events. There were three benches along the judge's side of the river and at each one as he passed he would leave two of the rods propped up against the bench and then move off down to the next one, where he did the same. At the last bench he sat down and lit a cigarette and smoked it as he watched the river. A few minutes later he obviously had seen a trout rise, so he grabbed one of the rods and started to work out some line and presented his fly over the fish. *So far so good*, I thought. He eventually rose and hooked the trout and played it out and netted it and then returned it to the water. The next rise was covered, and it rose to his fly and he tightened into it rather vigorously and contact was made, but he lost his fly to the fish. The judge dropped the rod and picked up his other rod, lengthened his line and carried on fishing. This routine continued all the way up the river until he arrived at the top pool which always held a good head of fish and last thing of an evening was a great spot to try a sedge fly, which he duly did. At no time did he tie on a fly to replace any lost flies during the entire session. As darkness fell, the judge collected up all his six rods and headed off to his house.

A few days later I met the judge in the village and asked him why he always took six rods to the river, even when I knew what his reasons were. His answer and explanation made simple common sense. He said his eyesight was so bad that he was unable to tie on a fly at the riverside, particularly evening times. He then explained his method that he had devised to overcome his eyesight problem and which enabled him to fish on without the worry of having to stop fishing altogether if he lost his fly in a fish.

He said he went into the local tackle shop and bought six cheap 8ft 6" 5 weight glass fibre rods and six cheap reels and six double tapered floating lines and a dozen 5x tapered Platil leaders. He then assembled all these rods and tied on his choice selection of flies using a magnifying glass under a bright light in his study. Whenever he went fishing he would take all six rods with him that were permanently kept made up and when not in use were propped up in the corner of his study. As and when he lost a fly, he said he would discard the flyless rod and take up another rod with a fly attached and continue fishing.

This method allowed the old judge to dry fly fish way into his eighties until he almost became totally blind and finally had to give up fishing. Good lateral thinking on the judge's part, I thought.

CHAPTER 5

A TALE OF A TAIL OF A BEAVER ON COLD CREEK IN ONTARIO

On one of my early visits to Canada, when I had been invited by the MNR (Ministry of Natural Resources Fisheries Dept.) to offer advice on headwater protection and restoration of wild trout habitat, I was invited one day to fish Cold Creek. This lovely little tributary of the River Trent system that flows into Lake Ontario on its north shore, was aptly named as it was mainly spring-fed out of the limestone glacial moraines that made up the majority of the catchment of this creek. Historically, fish-wise, it was originally naturally inhabited by indigenous North American brook trout in the head waters and with a good head of suckers and various types of chub in the warmer middle to lower reaches. Colonisation of the catchment by the first settlers and the cutting down of the dense forest of white pine and the opening up of the land to agriculture during the late eighteenth and throughout the nineteenth century, had taken its toll on the habitat of natural fish populations. As with many rivers in the UK, these rivers were treated solely as agricultural rivers where dams, weirs and mills powered by impounded water were built. The effect of these dramatic changes within the water course of the creek were that the natural fish life suffered.

Cold Creek had been identified by the scientists of the MNR as an ideal creek to restore as a self-sustaining brook trout stream. My small part in this restoration project was to bring my chalk stream experience of habitat protection and restoration to advise the fisheries' biologists involved on what needed to be done to restore suitable habitat that would enable the wild brook trout to regenerate naturally. Many of the rivers and stream that flow into Lake Ontario along the North Shore had been regularly stocked over the years with brown trout that were brought in from Germany and the UK during the 1880s and early 1900s. Remnants of these initial stockings did still maintain a foothold in some of these rivers. So brown trout were added to the list of species of fish that were to be protected and their populations restored.

However, this restoration project is not what this story is about – this story is my experience with a wild beaver on a day when I had been invited to fish while I was advising on Cold Creek. Advisory work can have its compensations!

I had been instructed to commence fishing above a disused mill and fish my way up the creek for about a couple of miles to an agreed point where we all were to meet sometime later in the day. It was July and it was a very hot day and as the vegetation and bank-side trees had been allowed to grow wild for many years, ploughing through the dense vegetation to get to the banks of the creek wearing chest waders alone was very exhausting and very quickly I was dripping with sweat. Chest waders were necessary as it was almost impossible to fish from the banks of the stream; one had to wade the stream to find a stretch of water where a cast could be made under or around the overhanging vegetation or under the alder trees that lined much of the banks. This was wilderness fishing in extremis! Nevertheless, I fished on up the creek and even managed to net a few small brook trout and one reasonable brown trout of about a pound in weight, all of which were safely returned. I had been informed earlier by one of the regular fly fishers who knew the water well to concentrate on the 'Tunnel' and that I would know the spot when I had got up to it.

I continued upstream and waded quietly round a bend and, yes, there it was, the 'Tunnel' just as described. It was a stretch of stream that was heavily lined with alder trees that had almost canopied the entire width of the creek at this point. My informant also said that there-in were some 'lunker' brown trout that lived amongst the roots of the alder trees whose roots protruded out from the banks under water. 'Lunkers' is a descriptive term used by Canadians and American fishermen to denote very big fish!

I crept up to the mouth of the 'Tunnel' and waited for something to rise. Although the alder canopy almost joined overhead, it was not so dense as to exclude some sunshine, so the dappled effect of the sun through the alder cover on to the flowing water was quite enchanting. Also, the canopy was just high enough to allow a careful dry fly cast to be made upstream if one waded carefully and kept an eye on the back cast! I was using that day an 8ft 4 weight Sage rod.

Nothing moved, so I waded quietly up the 'Tunnel' and stopped halfway through it and leaned on an overhanging branch of one of the alders. I parked my rod and rested a while and lit a cigarette and waited for something to rise. I must have stayed in that spot for at least half an hour as I took advantage of the shade and a cooling breeze that filtered down the tunnel and, without moving a muscle, my mind wandered off on other things as I observed and admired all the beauties of such a wild place. Suddenly my peace was shattered by a tremendous explosion right behind where I was standing up to my waist in water. It was as if someone had fired off a .303 rifle right beside my right ear... I almost jumped clean out of my waders with the sudden shock. When I had landed back into my waders I looked round to see a huge wild beaver not two yards from me, as he or she started to swim away downstream from me at some speed. I watched its bow wave disappear round the bend as it sped off in high dudgeon under water. "Gordon Bennett!" I think were the words I exclaimed, quite loudly!

I recounted my experience to the Ministry guys I met up with later in the day and they just fell about laughing. Unbeknown to me at the time, beavers have this habit of slapping the surface of the water with their huge flat and powerful tails, which creates a very loud crack. I learnt also that beavers use this as a danger warning signal to other beavers or as an alarm signal if they are taken by surprise. To this day I do not know which one of us – me or the beaver – was the first to be surprised.

Before you ask... no, I did not catch any 'lunkers' that day!

CHAPTER 6

THE ONE CAST SALMON WITH GARY COXON ON THE CRAIGOVER POOL ON TWEED AT MIDDLE MERTOUN

My great friend, Gary Coxon, had taken the fishing at Middle Mertoun and I had agreed to ghillie for him this particular day. I took him up to the Craigover Pool which I knew held some fish. He started to fish down the pool where deep wading was not needed, as it fishes well from the gravel bank and the whole width of the pool could be covered with ease. Gary fished down to the end of the pool as well as any good salmon fisher could – alas, not one salmon showed any interest, although some showed every few minutes or so, so we knew there were fish in the pool.

I suggested to Gary that he fish through the pool again using a smaller fly. Gary agreed and changed his fly as we walked back up the gravel bank. On reaching the top of the pool, Gary passed me his rod and said to have a chuck as he wanted to have a pee. I took his rod and started to let out some line for my first cast. Gary had by this time shed his jacket and was about to drop his waders when I made my first cast. The fly had hardly landed when I had a strong pull and on lifting the rod a strong salmon was on. Gary had hardly started his pee, let alone finished it! The ribald exclamations coming from behind the bush are unprintable! One cast, one salmon, I was happy... Gary was grumpy!

This is not the whole story; there is more to it than me catching a salmon first cast with Gary's rod as I had just done.

I played the fish out until eventually Gary was able to tail it out for me, and as it was a cracking fresh cock fish we decided to kill it. It was a spring week and at that time the second fish could be killed and as Gary had a fish the day before then we were not breaking the rules. Gary carried the salmon all of fifteen yards up the gravel bank and laid it down and just as he picked up a suitable stone to kill the fish it took off like greased lightning back to the river, still with the fly firmly attached to its mouth... We both stood and gasped in amazement as the fish sat upright and proceeded to swim all of the fifteen yards upright and without stopping and at great speed over the soft loose stones, spraying gravel each side of its body as it went, just as if it had been running through shallow water. On reaching the bank edge, it dived head first back into the river as if diving off a diving board. I managed to stoop down and grab the rod before the whole rod also followed the salmon into the river. I quickly let out some line and then gathered the line and renewed contact with fish. Luckily it was still well hooked and so I played out the fish once more. Gary, between fits of laughter by this time, tailed the salmon again but this time he was not going to make the same mistake, so he took the salmon twenty yards up the bank this time and did not release his hold on its tail until he had administered the *coup de gras* with a suitable rock!

Never ever have I seen or heard of a salmon swimming so far and so fast over dry gravel and head dive back into the river like an Olympic high board diver.

CHAPTER 7

DRY FLY ON LOCH CALLADAIL BY DURNESS BY CAPE WRATH. AND AN EMBARRASSING MEETING FOR A COUPLE IN THE BAR OF THE CAPE WRATH HOTEL

Several years ago, I received an invitation from a great friend of mine, John De Mora, to share a rod with him on the River Dionard (pronounced "Jinnard") way up by Cape Wrath which is about the farthest northwest one can get on the Scottish mainland. The Dionard River is well known for its salmon and grilse runs but being a spate river if one is to get some sport the water's flows have to be right.

I jumped at this invitation as I knew that there were also some excellent limestone lochs nearby to Durness that held excellent wild brown trout. I had read about Loch Calladail and the other lochs of the area, as their history has been well documented in angling literature.

The trip north was planned for the first week in September and we set off on the long drive from Hampshire to Cape Wrath. We did break the journey with an overnight stay in the Spey Valley, arriving early afternoon the next day at the Cape Wrath Hotel where we were booked in to stay for the week. That was my first visit to the very northwest of Scotland and on the drive north I wondered at the beauties of the autumn colours of the hills and mountains at that time of year; it was stunning scenery with the unique geology of the area epitomised by the white basalt outcrops contrasting with the autumn bracken and heather.

Mr Wilson was the owner of the hotel in those days and was very knowledgeable about all the fishing within a huge radius of the hotel. As we sat down for breakfast next morning, he came to the table to greet us and he asked where we were fishing. We replied that we were fishing the river Dionard for the week and also the limestone lochs if the river was out of order.

Mr Wilson said that although the Dionard was about five miles away, one could assess what the water conditions were like on the river Dionard without leaving the dining room we were then sat in. This puzzled us, but he soon explained when he had drawn our attention through the window and pointed towards hillside some four or five miles away. He asked if we could see the thin line of white water flowing steeply down the side of the said hill. We said it is just visible with a naked eye. Good, he said, the river is in good nick – get there now and fish it as soon as you can before it rains again. He followed on by saying that if the thin white line is not visible even with a pair of binoculars, then don't bother to fish: the river will be too low. If you can see the thin line of white water as it is today, then the river is in good order. If the white line of water is twice as wide as it is today and it stands out clearly, then the Dionard River is in spate so don't bother to go fishing on the river. The only chance of a grilse or two when the river is in spate is if one has access to fish Loch Dionard which is further up the river and is privately owned.

John and I fished the Dionard for the first couple of days, but the water dropped away and although we saw salmon we remained fishless. On the third day I decided to take my dry fly rod on to Loch Calladail and see what the wild brown trout were like. John said he would stick to the river, so he dropped me off beside the loch and left me to it for the day.

This part of Scotland is open to every breath of wind and with few trees and thousands of miles of the Atlantic to the west and north, rarely was there a day without a strong wind blowing. This morning I was lucky as there was a very light breeze from the west and there was a ten-yard area of flat calm around the shore of the lee side of the wind. *Good*, I thought, *that's where I will start*, so I walked around to the west side of the loch. I tackled up with my full Itchen dry fly set up, as to me this was the best tactic as the water was gin clear and a slight ripple had formed that rolled away from the bank which grew in size as it travelled across the loch. The start of the ripple was about ten yards out from the bank... again, *perfect*, I thought to myself. Well, my tactics proved right, as I had some great sport with a dry fly. I used a little upright winged Greenwell's Glory of my own long tailed tying on a size 18. This fly proved deadly in those conditions as I fished it in the calm, letting the floating fly be taken slowly into the ripple. Being a chalk stream fisher, most of my fishing in Hampshire is done on my hands and knees. With water in the loch being so clear, it had to be a hands and knees approach which proved quite painful on the knees that day due to the hard pebble and cobble banks of the loch and this proved right as I had to get upright quite often for a stretch and as and when I did the fish went down. And stopped rising. *Enough said*, I thought. During the day I killed a brace of good trout, both around a pound and half in weight, for breakfast for John and me next day and returned a dozen or more brown trout of various good sizes and all of good condition.

John picked me up at about five thirty and we headed back to the hotel where, after delivering my trout to the chef and giving instructions how we wanted them cooked, we went to the bar for a pint or three.

On entering the bar, it was empty of drinkers except for couple of uncertain age whispering sweet nothings into each other's ear in the darkest corner of the bar. I initially took little notice until my eyes had got used to the low light and I then recognised the couple in the corner. At the same second they both recognised me, but neither of them said a word to me as they both jumped up and rushed passed me out of the bar. I gather later from the hotel manager that the couple had just booked in for three nights but had suddenly changed their mind and had decided to leave... I wonder why... maybe because I knew who they were and that they were married, but not to one another, and both lived, but not together, not many miles from my house in Hampshire.

Now this couple were very unlucky, as who would have thought that after travelling all the way from Hampshire and staying in the most northerly hotel on the mainland of Scotland at Durness they would have the ill fortune to bump into someone from their home village! I kept their secret... I have often wondered if they ever knew that...

CHAPTER 8

POSH TOSH TREBLE TROUBLE

Treble hooks once firmly set in the mouth of a salmon rarely come adrift. The same could be said about treble hooks that get attached to other items like the back of a fishing jacket or the sleeve of a woollen jumper or, even worse, the back of one's neck or earlobe!

A year or so ago during the back end salmon fishing on Tweed, I was fortunate to have had a few days on the Mertoun waters. The morning after the last day's fishing, I drove into the village as usual to pick up my paper and buy my daily ration of cigarettes and get any items my wife required from the general stores. I was, as usual, wearing my tweed cap that I wear every day whether fishing or not, and like any fisherman, there are always a few flies attached to hat – all usually in a high state of deterioration. That day was no different, as during the previous day's fishing I had placed a size 8 treble dressed Posh Tosh into the very top of my hat when I was deep wading and wanted to change my fly down to a smaller size. Without thinking, I hooked the fly I had taken off into my hat, and I had not noticed that it was still there when I drove into the village.

I drew up the car outside of the paper shop and post office in the main street of St Boswells, but before I got out of the car I had to check that I had enough money in my pocket, so I tried to put my hand deep into my right-hand pocket to find some loose change. I have quite a small car so there is not a great deal of room in it, so when I tried to get my hand into my pocket I had to raise my whole body to ease my hand into my pocket. By raising my whole body, I pressed my head with my hat on hard against the roof lining of the car. I felt a searing pain on the top of my head and found when I tried to lower myself back down into my seat that my hat was firmly affixed to the roof lining of my car and my head firmly fixed to the inside of my hat by the barbs of a size 8 dressed treble Posh Tosh! I was almost suspended in mid-air by my scalp! What could I do, shout for help? No, people would only laugh. So, I gingerly drove home with a very stiff neck and some considerable pain. I hooted the horn of the car to attract the attention of my wife and she finally came out to see what the noise was all about. I told her what had happened and she fell about laughing, so I got no sympathy there; all she could do was to cut the barb out of the roof lining of the car so I could at least sit down and get out of the car. On close inspection, only one barb was caught in the roof lining, but the other two were well embedded way past the barbs, deep into my scalp, with my hat firmly fixed between the two. Although my wife had stopped laughing, she could not do anything to remove the hat and hook from my head. What should I do, drive all the way to A&E some six miles away? No, I will go down and see the head ghillie on the House Beat – so off I went. Luckily, he was there, and he asked what was wrong. I said, "Hook in Head" and pointed to my hat with a Posh Tosh on top and told him how it got there. Well, when he had picked himself off the floor laughing so much, he delved into his tool box of his big 4x4, pulled out a huge pair of rusty pliers and – carefully, I must admit – snipped off the Posh Tosh, so I could at least remove my cap, which just left two joined barbs of the treble still firmly embedded in my scalp. He took one look at the buried barbs and said no, he wasn't even going to try to remove those, even with a pair of rusty pliers. Go off to A&E at the BGH Borders General Hospital was his advice to me, so off I went. I went very sheepishly into reception and the nurse asked how she could help and I pointed to the top of my head and said, "Hook in head." She said, "Oh no, not another one, that's two today already!"

A doctor had a quick look and puffed a little anaesthetic spray on the offending area of my head and in one swift movement removed the two barbs in one single action... a dab of disinfectant and I was sent on my way with my tail between my legs and with a sore head.

CHAPTER 9

A YOUNG ANGLER'S FIRST SEA TROUT

Many more years ago than I wish to count, I well remember the first sea trout I caught. I was but a young teenager and was on a family holiday in South Devon, staying with a family friend who had a farm near Newton Abbot. Knowing that I was a keen angler, my host Colin arranged for me to go sea trout fishing one night with a local angler, Geoff, who was the local expert on sea trout fishing on the River Dart and who had access to some of the best sea trout waters on the Dart.

On the appointed day, Colin arranged for us to meet up with Geoff at lunchtime in a pub near to the water we were to fish that evening. After a chat and a couple of pints we set off and parked in a field close to the river. Geoff told me that we would park at this spot later that night and he was now going to show me where exactly I was to fish that evening. The day was bright and warm and typical for a day in Devon in late July. As we walked down the field towards the river, Geoff said – pointing to a large oak tree – that by that rock beside the oak tree would be my first cast tonight. I looked at the river which was quite low and very clear and although not gin clear like the chalk streams I knew, the water had a distinct cold-tea-without-milk look to it. I remarked on the colour of the water and Geoff said the colour came from the peat stratas over which the upper reaches of the river flow. I could see every stone and cobble across the whole riverbed except for a narrow deeper dark run along the far bank. There was not a fish in sight except for small groups of trout fry that scattered over the shallow waters under my feet along my side of the pool.

Geoff told me to look at my back cast space as I stood beside the rock where my first cast was to be made. I made a few pretend casts with my arm and mentally noted the space behind me. This I did several times and reckoned I could reach the far bank quite easily if I avoided the branches of the big oak tree. Down we went for a few yards and we stopped by a tree stump where Geoff said would be my position for my next cast that evening. Here was a good pool, I thought, but there was not a single fish to be seen, as every stone and pebble was so easy to see in the clear water. So, we proceeded down the river for about 500 yards with me mentally trying to remember where my back cast would go, to avoid the trees at all the casting points that Geoff had indicated to me. Walking back to the car, Geoff said that when we came back in the evening it would be very dark as there was no moon that night, so it was vital I remembered where all the casting points were. I thought to myself that it surely does not get that dark in Devon in late July... how wrong that thought was, which I would soon learn that evening!

Geoff dropped me back at the farm and we arranged for him to pick me up about ten o'clock that evening, which he duly did, and we drove off to the same pub we had visited earlier in the morning and sat down for a pint. I was anxious to get to the river and fish, but no, another pint arrived and we sat and talked some more about fishing. 10.30 arrived and I kept looking at my watch, yet Geoff seemed in no hurry to move. 11 o'clock arrived and last orders at the bar were called, so up came another pint! The regulars started to disperse and still we sat talking! At about 11.30 we eventually ambled over to the car and drove off to the river and parked in the same spot as we had done in the morning. I soon put up my rod and reel and Geoff produced the leader that I was to use that night... 8 foot of 7lb nylon. My rod was a split cane two-piece 9-foot Hardy Palakona Perfection and on the Hardy Perfect reel was a plaited Kingfisher silk line. So, this dates me as it was before glass fibre and carbon rods became popular! Geoff attached to my leader a blue black and silver dressed fly which was his own pattern that he had tied himself on a size ten single hook and the name of which escapes me now.

By this time it was almost midnight and still Geoff was not ready to approach the river. He leaned on the roof of the car, slowly recharging his pipe, saying that we should give it a few more minutes yet before we creep down to the river. My excitement was such that I was fit to burst by this time!

As we walked down the field into the narrow river valley towards the big oak tree, it became darker and darker as we went, and by the time we had arrived beside the big oak tree I could hardly make out the bank on the far side of the river and, in fact, I tripped over the rock from where I had been instructed to make my first cast.

After waiting for a few more minutes, Geoff whispered to me to make my first cast across the river and pitch my fly as near to the far bank as I could and let it come around with the current. Casting in almost complete darkness was a completely new experience to me as a complete beginner to night-time sea trout fishing. However, once I had got my timing right I managed to get my fly to the right spot.

 Try lengthening a line and aerialising twenty yards of line and casting with your eyes closed or blindfolded and you will soon realise how much one subconsciously watches the line to maintain the right timing of the cast when fishing during the light of day! I was on a steep learning curve. No joy at the first pool; it was surely my bad casting that put the fish off. We moved quietly down to the next stance and tried again. This time I felt a pluck, but Geoff said that it was probably a small brown trout and after several casts, each one evoking small plucks, we moved on to the next pool. By this time my eyes had become accustomed to the darkness and I could make out the far bank reasonably well, although to me it was almost pitch black.

Suddenly, half way down the next pool, all hell let loose as my rod was almost snatched out of my hand and the reel screamed as a fish ran away with my fly. Gathering my wits and all the loose line, I eventually made contact with the fish and had it on the reel. The fight was mind blowing for me, as I was unable to control this fish. At one point my rod and line were pointing downstream and suddenly a fish jumped clear of the water some few yards above me... *no, that could not be my fish*, I thought, but realised it was as my line cut through water past me with that unmistakable sound. I was convinced that this had to be salmon by the way it fought with such power for its freedom. After what seemed a long time but only could have been a minute or two, I managed to beach the fish and Geoff tapped it on the head and shook my hand and congratulated me on my very first sea trout. As I, in silent reverence, admired the trout as it lay on the gravel, it appeared to be iridescent as its silver body shone so brightly in the darkness of the river bank. It was a beautiful creature. That was it; I had achieved what I set out to do: catch a sea trout.

Back at the car, Geoff weighed the fish in the headlights, and much to my surprise it was only three and half pounds. I was convinced when playing the fish that it must be eight to ten pounds by the way it fought with such strength and the strain it exerted on my tackle. How can such a small fish fight so hard? Nevertheless, I was very happy with my three and half pounds and although I have been fortunate to have caught larger sea trout since, the memories of that fish and that river and every minute of that wonderful day and night have lived with me ever since. That is the way with sea trout fishing!

CHAPTER 10

FISHING THE MURRELL ON THE HELMSDALE AND MY INTRODUCTION TO DIBBLING FOR SALMON BY JOHNNIE HARDY ON THE ALDER RUN

In the early nineties I was very fortunate to have been invited by a good friend to fish for three days as his guest on the Helmsdale river, which, for me, is one of the best (if not *the* best) salmon rivers in Scotland; if not the best, it is certainly one of the most attractive rivers to fish. We were staying at Borribol Lodge, and the ghillie was that well-known and greatly respected Helmsdale ghillie and scratch golfer Johnnie Hardy, who has since unfortunately retired.

The first morning, my host directed Johnnie to take me down to fish the Murrell Pool, which is the first pool up from the Association water above the village of Helmsdale.

On arrival, we parked up in a layby that overlooked the pool I was to fish. Johnnie directed me down the path to the top of the pool and told me where to start and how far down to fish. He said he would return as soon as he had taken another rod to start further up the river. I fished the pool down and managed to take one fresh fish of about eight pounds. Johnnie returned and stood on a rock above the pool and watched as I fished. He was very intent, as he was wearing Polaroid glasses and was shielding his glasses with his hands as he concentrated on the water I was fishing. On reaching the end of the pool, he directed me to come out of the river so we could move on to the next pool. As I arrived back up to where the car was parked, Johnnie said I was fishing over a hundred salmon. He said to come and have a look, so with my Polaroid glasses on I could just make out a huge shoal of salmon lying evenly throughout the pool I had just fished down. He said that I had fished well, but as I worked my way down the pool the salmon slowly backed away from me and when I had almost reached the end of the pool, the salmon started to move back past me and lined up behind me upstream. Some fish passed by me on both sides and all within a foot or two of my waders where I was standing in the river, but I was completely oblivious of what was happening. For all I knew, there had been only one fish in the pool and I had caught that one! It is not often one can see shoals of salmon when one is fishing, but the light conditions and clarity of water that morning made it possible to see these fish. How many times have we fished through a pool and not had a fish, let alone a pull, when in fact we have just fished over a hundred salmon? Many times, I suspect.

Johnnie took me upstream to the Alder tree run, which was a narrow run between two wider pools and at the present height of water he said it was ideal to try dibbling for a salmon. I had heard of and had read accounts of this method but had never seen it used or tried it myself. I was intrigued to say the least. I was using a 13ft 6inch 9 weight two-handed salmon rod that day, with a full floating line and a tapered leader of about ten feet. Johnnie took my fly off and tied on a small but heavy tube fly without a hook on the point, but two feet above the point he tied a dropper on to my leader upon which he tied small size 14 double hook sea trout fly, sparsely tied with blue and silver stoat tail hair. He took my rod and as he stood beside the narrow run he placed the heavy point fly on the beach on the far side of the run, which was only about 15ft wide at this point where the white water was rushing down the run only a few inches to a foot deep. He drew the weighted fly into the flow and holding the rod high he bounced the dropper fly across the run from wave top to wave top until it reached the near bank. He repeated this action for me and then handed the rod to me and directed me to copy that action down every foot of the run. I must admit, I thought that no self-respecting salmon would take that fly as the water was so shallow, and I wondered how a salmon could see the fly in the turbulent white water. However, after a few casts a salmon poked his head out of the white water and firmly took hold of the dropper fly that was just under my rod tip, bouncing wave top to wave top and almost at my feet! The fish ran off downstream and I played it out in the pool below, where Johnnie netted it out. *Wow*, I thought to myself, *that must have been a fluke*, but Johnnie told me to go back and carry on dibbling down the run, and by the time I had reached the end I had taken three more salmon all in the same identical way! From then on I was hooked on dibbling! It was incredible and so exciting to see a salmon take so close and in such shallow water taking a small fly that was almost in the air! An unforgettable experience and a most memorable day.

CHAPTER 11

SALMON AND A PUBLIC FOOTBRIDGE

Talking about spotting salmon in a river reminds me of a day on my own water on the Itchen, when and where I was the river keeper before I retired. There is a public footbridge that runs across the river, half way up our middle beat. The path to and from this bridge joined the two villages of Easton on the south side and Martyr Worthy on the north side of the river. The bridge was a popular meeting place not only for the locals but for many of the hikers and walkers that used the valley, as it provided a good view of the river upstream and downstream.

One particular day, during a September, I happened by and as there were half a dozen walkers stood admiring the view, I introduced myself as the keeper of this beat of the river and they started to ask me questions about the river and wildlife etc. This I have always been happy to do, as I believe it is important to share my knowledge of the river with other people.

One question that was asked was "Are there any salmon in the Itchen and do they come up this far in the river?" I became a bit wary at this point as such knowledge, if it got into the wrong hands, could spell trouble! I told the group that yes, salmon do come into the Itchen, but I have not seen one in this part of the river for several years and left it at that. Other questions were asked and the group then moved on along the path towards Easton.

Unbeknown to them, if they had looked under their feet and through the gaps in the decking boards of the bridge while they stood on the footbridge, they would have seen three salmon hiding there. I had watched these salmon for several days and they seemed quite happy where they were, even though the bridge was used regularly, and despite the noisy trampling of the feet of many people passing over their heads each day, just 18 inches above their heads, as the river was no more than two-foot-deep at any point under the footbridge. They stayed there for another week or two, until they moved on to spawn further up the river. As far as I knew, no one ever did get to know they were there. Although I did keep a close eye on them to ensure the local 'bad boys' did not spot them!

CHAPTER 12

RATTLERS AND COPPERHEAD SNAKES ON THE RIVER LE TORT IN PENNSYLVANIA

On one of my earliest trips to the USA, I was invited by the Pennsylvania Fisheries Commission to have look at the habitat restoration work Charlie Fox had undertaken on his stretch of one of the famous limestone creeks, called The Le Tort, in the Cumberland Valley at Carlisle near to Harrisburg. I remember it well as it was almost twelve months after the almost disastrous Three Mile Island nuclear incident when an atomic reactor in a generation station on Three Mile Island went into meltdown. Fortunately, a major nuclear disaster was averted.

Charlie Fox had been working hard for several years restoring and maintaining the spawning habit for the resident brown trout population of the Le Tort. The main problems were due to major land use changes over the years in the catchment and the effects of large and poorly regulated commercial watercress farming operations on the upper reaches of the creek. The once prolific spawning facilities for these resident populations of brown trout and native brook trout had been almost destroyed. Although there were still quite a few very big brown trout surviving in the creek, the younger year classes of both species were obvious by their absence. The weed life consisted of mainly *Elodea* (Canadian pond weed) and annual watercress with a few clumps of portamento, all of which, except for the portamento, grew in great profusion along the creek margins. In places, the growths were such that it almost covered the entire creek bank to bank. The creek looked very sorry for itself as I was to learn after talking to Charlie Fox, who showed me photographs of the creek when it was in its prime some years prior to my visit.

On the appointed day for me to meet Charlie Fox, he had also invited a fellow friend and fellow fly fisherman. That friend turned out to be that well-known dry fly angler and author Vince Marinaro of *In the Ring of the Rise* fame, who, like Charlie, had been born and reared in the Cumberland Valley and, like Charlie, had also cut his teeth dry fly fishing for wild brown trout and brook trout on the limestone creeks of the Cumberland Valley. Charlie's property and his back yard stretched right down to the edge of the creek, where Charlie had positioned, on a small knoll under the shade of a large tree, a very rustic but comfortable bench, from which when sat upon afforded a good view of the creek, both upstream and down.

The three of us sat down on the bench and during the following hour or so I listened intently as Charlie and Vince related to me the fishing history of the Le Tort and as they recounted all the land use changes and detrimental happenings that had, in their opinion together, culminated in the virtual destruction of the trout populations and trout habitat of the creek.

Charlie was keen to show me the work he had done on the creek, particularly his new spawning channels he had constructed with imported local gravel and the natural stone and cobble of the creek bed. To get to these areas we had to wade up the creek or fight our way through the dense vegetation that grew along both banks, so Charlie loaned me a pair of thick waders. It was August and it was hot and very humid – in fact I was to learn later that the temperature at midday that day was 96 F and the humidity stood at 90%! It was a 'Ninety-Ninety' day, as the locals called it. I suffered that afternoon as I followed Charlie and Vince up the creek.

I can stand high temperatures as long as there is low humidity... it's the humidity that slays me. I really thought I was going to die that afternoon.

As a casual aside Charlie warned me, as we tramped on, to look out for rattle snakes and copperhead snakes. Not being a great lover of snakes at the best of times, I was suddenly glad to be wearing some thick waders, despite the searing heat and debilitating humidity. It was not long before Charlie pointed to a large rattler curled up on a bank of shingle, sunning itself beside the creek. "Don't worry," he said, as he casually lobbed a large stone in its direction, making the rattler indignantly shake its rattle as it woke up and slid away into the bankside vegetation.

A rattler's rattle is an unmistakable sound never to be forgotten once one has heard it for the first time. That was my first time and I have not forgotten that sound! Vince said that all one has to do if you come across a rattler when you are fishing is, firstly, avoid treading on it and then poke it with your rod tip; it will then go away, as rattlers are more frightened of you than you are of them... *Yeah,* I thought to myself, *you might think and do that, but I know thousands who wouldn't!*

Copperheads are slightly different, Vince went on to say. They are a smaller snake and obviously named by their bright copper colour. Their venom is far more powerful than a rattler, so a bite from a copperhead has to be treated very quickly or else it could be fatal. I tramped on, swallowed hard and said nothing!

All the local hospitals carry adequate stocks of snakebite serum, so don't worry, Vince assured me, which gave me some comfort. I told him that back home on the Itchen I have heard grown men squeal with fright when they have noticed a slow worm on the banks of the river! I went on to say that we did not have any poisonous snakes on the chalk streams, only a few smooth snakes and grass snakes, both of which were perfectly harmless. Only on the acid ground away from the chalk lands would we find the adder, and this species is the only poisonous snake we have in UK. An adder can give one a painful bite but rarely, if ever, is an adder bite life threatening if treated quickly (within an hour or two).

During my enjoyable stay in the Cumberland Valley I was privileged to fish not only the Le Tort but also two other well-known limestone creeks: Boiling Springs and Yellow Breeches. Great names for fishing creeks, are they not? However, all the time I was fishing these creeks and being a soft Brit, I had great difficulty concentrating on my fishing, as I was subconsciously keeping an eye out for rattlers and copperheads with every step I made.

CHAPTER 13

AN AQUATIC MAD MARCH HARE

It was part of my daily routine every morning to exercise my kennel full of spaniels in the fields beside the top beat of the river. My route to the fields was to walk down my garden onto the river bank and walk upstream to the top beat footbridge which I had to cross to get to the regular spaniel exercise field. This particular morning, I was just approaching the footbridge with five spaniels walking obediently at heel, when one of them suddenly dived off the narrow footpath into the thick sedge. Out popped a fully grown hare, which bolted up the path in front of the rest of the spaniels, closely followed by the first spaniel that had put up the hare. I shouted "No!", "Come to Heel!" and some other unprintable expletives at the top of my voice but to no avail. Within a trice, not to lose out on a bit of fun, the other spaniels burst into action and followed the first spaniel at top speed as only spaniels can! What came to mind was the warning that any good spaniel trainer must know: 'Always be aware of the hare'. Oh well, it's their exercise time and just one hare hunt won't do much harm. I watched as the hare sped up the river bank with five spaniels in close pursuit, until it arrived at a sharp left-hand bend of the river. I thought the hare would turn the corner and follow the bank path up the next beat. Not a bit of it. When the hare reached the bend it did not hesitate or break step or turn the corner, it took off and leapt a good ten or twelve feet out into the river, just like an Olympic long jumper. It landed in the water with such a force that it submerged for a few seconds, before it poked its head above the water and proceeded to swim powerfully towards the far bank. The spaniels screeched to a halt and just stared at the swimming hare. I am sure I noticed an amazed expression on all their faces as they watched the hare haul itself out of the river onto the river bank, where it stopped and sat up to shake out the excess water. It then turned around to see where the spaniels were before it ran off into the field.

I now joined in the fun as I whispered to the spaniels, "Get on." The spaniels knew that command and they knew where the footbridge was, so they all turned around without being told and ran back down the bank to where the footbridge was and ran over the bridge and headed up the far bank to the place where the hare had hauled itself out of the river. They all milled about in the field, until one spaniel picked up the scent of the hare and soon decided in which direction the hare had gone. The hunt was still on. The spaniels quartered the field for some minutes, but with not a sign of the hare. After a few minutes, I whistled the spaniels back to heel and all obeyed, except one who was busily working some thick grass some hundred yards away. With four spaniels panting hard but sat to heel, I watched as the other spaniel busily worked the grass until *whoops* out popped the hare. *Tally-ho, here we go again,* I thought, as the spaniel closed in on the hare. My other spaniels could not see what was happening as the grass was too high, so although they were eager I managed to hold them at heel as I watched events out in the field. The chasing spaniel was closing in, but the hare was heading straight back towards the river and was just about holding its own for speed. No, it could not happen again, I said to myself. It did! The hare dived under the fence without breaking step, onto the river bank, and without slowing down it again launched itself headlong out into the river and swam to the other bank. My other spaniels heard the splash, but as they couldn't see the action they were not tempted to join in the fun. The hare again hauled itself out of the river and again shook itself, turned to look where its pursuer was and ambled off into the thick sedge beds. The chasing spaniel stood on the far bank wondering whether to follow the hare, but fortunately it obeyed my whistle and trotted back to join its mates!

A few minutes later, I noticed a very bedraggled hare hopping slowly up the field beyond the sedge beds. I quietly whispered to myself, "Good girl, didn't she do well!"

CHAPTER 14

THE WILTSHIRE BUDGIE!

For well over twenty seasons, I worked my spaniels picking up on the famous Druids Lodge partridge and pheasant shoot on the edge of Salisbury Plain, a mile from Stonehenge in Wiltshire. One particular incident stands out in my memory and always brings a smile to my face whenever I recall the story: the day when one of my spaniels appeared out of some cover and nudged me in the back of my leg. On turning and looking down I could see she had something small in her mouth which was certainly not a partridge. I offered my hand and she gently deposited into it a bright blue budgerigar which was dead but had not been dead very long, as its body was cold and rigor mortis had only just set in. The bird had not been shot but most probably was an escapee that had died of the cold and lack of food.

I duly passed it over to the guys who manned the game cart and they, with great mirth, ceremoniously tied it up with a partridge to make a brace and hung it on the rail in the game cart. I heard next day that the budgie was officially recorded in the estate game book records for the day under 'sundries'. The mixed brace was also presented with much hilarity at the end of the day to one of the guns who was a guest of the host with the words, "I believe these belong to you sir, they were picked up behind you after the second drive!"

CHAPTER 15

THE PERFECT START TO A GAME SHOOTING CAREER

The Peter of 'white string' fame, although very experienced as a trout and salmon fisher who had fished for Atlantic salmon in many parts of the northern hemisphere where Atlantic salmon run, informed me one day that he had decided to take up traditional English driven game shooting. This was a sport of which he had little or no experience. He sought my advice on how he should start. I told him that he should take a series of shooting lessons from a qualified expert shooting instructor. Fortunately, there was a well-known shooting school near Andover run by David Olive, who was a world class clay shooter and a fully qualified shooting instructor. Peter booked a series of lessons. He made time to spend at least two whole days per week, from early spring through to early summer, taking lessons from David Olive. It must have cost Peter a fortune.

Peter and David became good friends and Peter would bring David to the river to fish and share a wine or two!

While fishing, I would ask David how Peter was getting on with his shotgun skills and the answer was good: Peter was a good pupil and is now shooting well and is safety aware. That was good news.

CHAPTER 16

ADVENTURE WITH A PORCUPINE IN THE WILDS OF ONTARIO

After completing my work with the MNR (Ministry of Natural Resources) in Ontario one year, a couple of experienced fishermen invited me to accompany them on a three-day fishing trip up into the wilds of central Ontario to explore and fish some wild rivers. This was an invitation I could not refuse! Having driven north for some hours along unmade-up tracks beyond the Algonquin Park, we eventually stopped beside a large lake called Lake Lasswade. Here we made base camp and brewed up coffee. The surroundings were pure Canadian wilderness. I was told that there was a nice river that flowed into the lake which held a good population of brook trout and that would be the river we were to fish. As there were no roads or tracks around the lake shore, we would have to walk into this river through dense forest which would take about three hours. Being late in the afternoon, we decided to make that river our destination the following day, so we leisurely made our camp for the night on the lake shore. As it was only late April, the nights were quite cold - in fact, very cold despite a roaring log fire! Being experienced backwoodsmen, my friends soon had the coffee brewing again and we feasted on some huge succulent steaks cooked over the log fire and we washed this meal down with strong black coffee laced with some Famous Grouse whisky. The evening became colder as we talked around the fire, each taking a turn at throwing on another log to keep the blaze going. I soon learnt that one did not undress to go to bed in these conditions! All one did was take off your boots and climb into a sleeping bag fully clothed, making sure your boots were near to the fire so they would not freeze solid! Adequately topped up with steak and whisky-laced coffee, sleep came easily! I awoke with the luxurious smell of bacon being cooked over the fire. In such wilderness there is nothing better than hot bacon rolls and strong black coffee for breakfast. After breakfast, my friends packed up camp and hoisted the bags up into a large tree and left them suspended so as not to attract the black bears that frequent the forest and who were just coming out of hibernation at this time of year. The bears would be very hungry and would have torn all our bags asunder if there was the slightest whiff of food in them if we had left them on the ground whilst we were away fishing. I was on a very steep learning curve regarding survival in the Canadian backwoods!

With all the morning camp chores completed, we donned our waders and put up our rods and made off to the river. As we tramped through the woods we talked loudly and made a good deal of noise so as to scare off any bears who might be in the area. This seemed to work as we did not see any bears on our journey, but we did put up quite a few wood grouse.

About two and a half hours later we arrived at the river. It looked good to me and I took some photographs while we decided where were going to fish. I was directed to go upstream and explore the river and fish where I could find casting space. I soon found a good pool and started to fish with a team of smallish wet flies as directed, as there were no insects hatching at this time of year. Within a few minutes I felt that something was not quite right with my rod and with my casting. It was a cloudless blue sky, the air was clear - very dry and still - and the sun felt quite warm on my face and after the long walk I was quite warm in my body. I reeled in to check my rod and line only to find that the rings of my rod were clogged with ice. I dipped my rod into the water to clear the ice, but no sooner had I started to cast again the rings clogged up with ice almost immediately. Although it did not feel cold at all, the temperature must have been below freezing. As it was still quite early in the day I decided to stop fishing and wait for the air temperatures to rise and in the meantime take some photographs of the beautiful scenery. I spotted a huge rock ahead of me which stood some twenty-foot-high, from the top of which I thought would give me a good view of the river, both upstream and downstream. I parked my rod and climbed up onto the rock and sat down to enjoy the scene and the warmth of the sun. I must have been there for almost an hour just taking in the scene, watching the river and generally relaxing and taking the odd photograph. My attention was suddenly taken by a crashing sound in the woods away to my left. It sounded to me like an elephant ploughing its way through the thick undergrowth and it was heading in my direction. My immediate thought was that it was a black bear... what shall I do, other than panic? My friends were way down river and I doubt if they would have heard if I had shouted, as the sound of the flowing river would have drowned out my shout for help. *Keep calm,* I kept telling myself, but not very convincingly I must admit. Shall I get off my perch high on the rock and climb a tall tree? No... black bears can climb trees better than I can, so I decided to stay where I was, and I told myself to keep quiet and wait events. The crashing noises came inexorably closer and closer, until I could see the small trees and undergrowth being pushed aside. I held my breath, lit yet another cigarette to calm my nerves and stared transfixed at the moving undergrowth. Eventually the beast broke cover and to my surprise and great relief my imaginary black 'bear' showed itself to be the biggest porcupine I had ever seen in my life. It must have been all five-foot-tall from its tallest quill to the ground. The animal ambled towards the rock I was perched up upon and looked up at me for a few seconds with a pair of very bloodshot eyes and then proceeded to pee against the rock... *Huh! That's what he thinks of me,* I thought to myself, as he or she ambled off down the river bank with its quills rattling loudly as it went on its way.

I did not fish with a great deal of enthusiasm or concentration for the rest of the day. Particularly as I instinctively kept both ears cocked for any unexplained sounds from the adjacent woods. My fishing companions just fell about laughing when I recalled my experiences with the porcupine over supper that night. They assured me that black bears rarely attack humans; they will go out of their way to avoid humans when they hear humans approaching. Females with cubs can be very protective and dangerous if humans try to get too close. Generally, if bears are left alone and given a wide berth they will not bother humans. However, if a fisherman catches and kills a good fish and it is left on the river bank close to where the fisherman is fishing and there is a bear in the area and he winds the dead fish, he very well may strongly dispute the ownership of that dead fish with the angler! Don't argue, just back off and allow the bear to take the fish. Bears much prefer raw fish flesh to raw humans. A good argument for the promotion of catch and release of trout and salmon, methinks!

The following day we moved on to another river and I did manage to net a few nice brook trout which we grilled over the log fire and shared for supper that evening. All in all, a great wilderness experience in some beautiful places with great wildlife.

CHAPTER 17

THE UPPER ITCHEN AT ITS MOST FRUSTRATING BEST

In my early days as a river keeper at Martyr Worthy on the upper Itchen, the tradition was that every alternate weekend there would be house guests staying at the 'Big House'. It was summertime and these guests were fishing guests. Normally the party would arrive at the Big House in late afternoon of the Friday and after settling in they would all adjourn down to the river to set up rods for the weekend and have a brief look at the river and maybe have a cast or two. After chatting to me and asking for all the latest information of how the river had been fishing and what flies I would suggest they used over the next two days, they would then all return to the Big House for pre-dinner drinks.

As the Big House was noted for the quality of its wine cellar, few, if any, fisher house guests would appear on the river after dinner on the Friday evening!

Saturday morning at about 10am, the guests would arrive at the fishing hut and after discussions as to who fished where on the river they would disperse and go their separate ways to fish. As river keeper I was available to help all the guests. If not specifically required to ghillie for one of the guests, I would keep an eye on all the fishermen and help whenever required.

Having set the scene, there was one particular day that stands out in my memory when there were just two guests fishing the Saturday evening rise after they had taken an early dinner.

The conditions were perfect in so much as there was broken cloud, no wind, and the evening rise was in full swing when the rods started fishing. Trout were moving steadily to spinners and the odd dun of the medium olive and the BWO. The upstream migration of clouds of BWO (blue-winged olive) were a sight to behold, as the air was thick with these egg-laden flies as they passed in a constant stream over my head as I stood on one of the footbridges. They were on their egg laying flight upstream to lay their eggs in some faster flowing streams of the beats above us. I took a sample by wafting my hat over my head and at each pass I collected many of these insects for inspection and then let them all go. These were all females of the BWO and each fly had a ball of green eggs tightly tucked under their bodies. Silhouetted against the setting sun, there appeared to be a fog over the river created by the huge number of BWO flighting upstream – a wonderful sight of nature working.

I sent the fishermen to the bottom of the beat with the instructions to start to fish opposite one another upstream from the footbridge and for them to work up the beat at their own speed. The river is wide enough for two fly fishers to fish opposite each other, but never do two anglers fish at the same speed, so one soon had worked his way further upstream whilst the other fished a little slower. The trout were rising steadily... *perfect evening rise,* I thought to myself, as I sat on the handrail of a footbridge to watch.

After about half an hour, "What are these damned trout taking?" was a call from one of the fisherman.

"Try a Sherry Spinner size 18," I replied.

"I have tried that fly," was a response from the other bank. "I am on a Lunn's Particular at the moment, but they don't want to know."

So, the evening progressed as the fishermen slowly worked their way up the river and steadily worked their way through the many patterns of fly they had in their fly boxes, each covering good trout that were steadily rising as they progressed. The language across the river deteriorated as the evening wore on, and the light was fading fast, and still no fish had been touched, let alone caught.

Having reached the end of the beat, the two fisherman called it a day and walked out onto the footbridge, at the middle of which I was sat on the handrail. Fly boxes were opened and both anglers discussed all the various patterns and sizes of fly they had tried that evening. "Why wouldn't these fish take tonight?" I was asked.

I tried to be tactful in my reply and answered, "That's the Itchen for you, the wild trout of the upper Itchen can be like this sometimes; they are noted for it. Even Mr Halford found the wild trout of this part of the river almost impossible to catch at times – that's why he refused some invitations to fish it! Even the likes of Dermot Wilson, who is regarded as the best dry fly fisherman on the upper Itchen, would have the odd blank evening on this beat."

To help soften their frustrations I recalled something that Dermot Wilson had told me some years before – that if this beat was not fished for the whole season, the wild trout would still be very difficult to catch... how right he was! Somehow this reply still did not appease their obvious frustrations.

I had, over many seasons at Martyr Worthy, closely watched evening rises when fish were rising all over the river. I have observed trout feeding and although they take a fly off the surface sometimes they would allow twenty or fifty naturals float by and not lift their heads. They would even lift to a natural dun or spinner and almost touch it with their noses for a few seconds while they drifted down a few feet in the current, inspecting each natural fly very closely and then refuse to take it and turn away and return to their feeding lie. What chance has the fly fisherman when the trout are so pernickety as that? I could even see the trout's eyes tuned inwards as if they were naturally cross-eyed, as they inspected each natural fly so closely before they rejected the natural fly.

The fabled evening rise is not always a productive time to catch trout, especially on the upper Itchen. Evening time at the end of a summer's day on the banks of the Itchen can be a magical place to be among all the abundant insect life and the sounds of the wildlife and the heavy scents of the wild flowers and dank sedge beds filling the air. If the trout are less choosy, then good sport can be had, but do not expect the same the next time you fish the evening rise on the Itchen!

After a long discussion between the two anglers who stood on the footbridge, one of them opened his fly box again, a box which must have held a hundred or more dry flies of assorted patterns suitable for the Itchen. He slowly turned the box upside down and emptied the entire contents onto the surface of the river as it flowed under the footbridge. I watched in astonishment as he tapped out the last fly in the box. Nothing was said as we watched the artificial hatch of assorted flies drift off downstream and down a run between two beds of *Ranunculus*, where some rising trout had been spotted earlier. The river immediately erupted as several good-sized trout rose with some alacrity and without any hesitation confidently took nearly every artificial fly that floated down!

"Well, that just proves it," said the fisherman. "The flies I used were OK, it must have been the idiot at the other end that was to blame for a blank evening!"

With that, they bade me goodnight and returned to the Big House to drown their sorrows, no doubt!

CHAPTER 18

'TIME WASTERS' CORNER' MY FAVOURITE DRY FLY POOL

If asked which is my favourite pool to fish with a dry fly, it must be 'Time Wasters' Corner' on the Chilland beat of the River Itchen at Martyr Worthy, where I was, until retirement, most privileged to have been the river keeper for almost thirty years.

This pool is so aptly named, as over the years many an angler has spent many an hour, and on many an occasion the whole day, on hands and knees trying to coax the wily wild brown trout residents that made this spot their home, to rise to their artificial.

This corner is a natural 90-degree bend in the river where the flow turns this corner at some speed for a chalk stream, and as it does so it increasingly splays out as it flows around the corner, giving a variety of ever-changing current speeds as it proceeds round and heads downstream. Each delicately presented cast invites the dreaded drag no matter how one used and tried all the various well-known slack line casts that professional AAPGAI instructors try to teach us!

As the dry fly lands upstream of the rising fish, the current takes hold immediately, but at this point the flow moves in two directions at the same time: firstly and naturally downstream, but also it moves across the river, slowing down as it progresses. No matter what angle the line and leader is cast to cover fish, every downstream drift of six inches includes three inches of sideways drift. The drag thus formed is horrific, and even a good slack line cast would only present the fly without drag for a mere inch or two! As soon as drag took hold, the wily resident trout ignored the artificial and continued, with very annoying and arrogant alacrity, sipping every natural fly that passes over them.

These resident wild trout are very free risers and clearly visible to the observant hidden angler kneeling behind the fringe on the river bank, and these trout seemed to know that they were completely safe from danger. Even the slightest hint of drag by an artificial fly in the gin-clear water would be ignored by these trout, and neither would drag frighten or deter the trout from continuing to feed avidly on naturals, unless a real splashy presentation was made. One almost sensed the trout were taking the Michael by cynically putting two fins in the air to the angler!

'Time Wasters' Corner' has to be, for me, the most challenging, frustrating and yet exciting casting on any chalk stream anywhere in the UK or perhaps the world. Over the years I have watched many expert dry fly fishers tackle this pool, mostly without a great deal of success, but to a man all have come away with the comment at close of play that it is the best and most challenging casting they have experienced. Yet success can be achieved on 'Time Wasters' Corner' else it would not have attained such notoriety. Other than using a delicate unweighted upstream nymph (size 18 PTN) to a nymphing trout, there is a possible chance of rising a trout to a dry fly if there is a downstream breeze blowing that gives a slight feathery ripple on the water surface, which can mitigate the visible effects of even the most minute hint of drag. This breeze also makes natural flies skate a little at times and it's these times when the observant angler may be in with a chance to fool a fish.

This beat has been recognised by many famous fishermen, including the legendary Sir Edward Gray, as the finest there is. This is underlined by the fact that the late Dermot Wilson, that doyen of chalk stream fishing who fished this beat for many years, requested in his will that his ashes be cast along the banks of the best stretch of chalk stream in the world: the banks of the Chilland beat of the River Itchen around 'Time Wasters' Corner'.

When last fishing this water just recently this summer, I had the distinct feeling that Dermot was looking down on me and smiling at my pathetic attempts to avoid the dreaded drag on 'Time Wasters' Corner'!

CHAPTER 19

I KNOW I AM A GRUMPY OLD MAN, BUT I AM OLD FASHIONED!

One of the most influential pieces of angling writing ever written about angling ethics and attitudes was encapsulated in an essay written by the late fly fisherman, writer and conservationist Ed Zern, which appeared in the *Field and Stream* some forty or more years ago, entitled 'The Ethics of Fly Fishing'. That essay, at the time, sowed the seeds within me from which have grown the present heartfelt feelings I have today concerning the wonderful sport of fly fishing which has been such an integral part of my life for the past fifty years or more – thirty years of which were spent as a river keeper on the upper River Itchen in Hampshire.

When given some thought, it seems that all the problems of life are ethical problems and so when attempting to separate out the ethics of fly fishing it is found to be rather difficult. Maybe, perhaps, it is not really ethics that are in mind but rather a one of attitudes, a code of behaviour, a concern for tradition and the preservation of fly fishing values and above all a desire for the conservation of our wild strains of trout and the rivers in which they live.

The essence of our sport of fly fishing in general, and dry fly fishing in particular, is skill and the voluntary imposition or acceptance of arbitrary conditions demanding these skills. There is nothing illegal in shooting a pheasant on the ground, but the true sportsman will only lift his gun to pheasants that are flying high and fast and even then may decline a shot which does not challenge his shooting skills.

Fly fishing usually requires more skills than fishing with metal spinners or heavy spoons; fly casting generally requires more skill than spinner casting or bait casting. Fly fishing encourages the development of collateral senses and skills, as in the powers of observation and the ability of identification of insects and the dexterity of tying accurate imitations of the same. Dry fly fishing hones the skills in adept field craft and encourages a stealthy stream approach and delicate fly presentation. Dry fly fishing can be a more sporting way of catching trout we see feeding off the surface of the water in which they live. If, at times, the spin, bait and the Czech-style nymph fisherman happens to catch more fish than the fly fisherman it is irrelevant because it could just be the other way around, but then who really cares?

The sport of fly fishing is surely not just a game or a hard-fought competition between fishermen – it is an end in itself. If we look at those great figures in the historical tradition of fly fishing, they are not the men who caught the largest fish or hold a vast array of cups and shields and medals for the greatest numbers caught in competitions. They are those men who, like Ronalds and Francis, Mottram and Sheringham, Halford, Marryat and Skues, Lord Gray of Falloden, Dermot Wilson, Theodore Gordon and Lee Wulff, Frank Sawyer, John Goddard and Vincent Marinaro and many others, gave to our sport lasting contributions of thought and knowledge, of the fish themselves, of fly fishing and fly fishing philosophy. All of which is set down in their writings and illustrated above all by their good sportsmanship.

There have always been those fishermen who could accumulate more fish in their catch returns than anyone else. They belong to a fraternity who have that overwhelming desire to be seen to have caught the most or largest fish. Why is this? Because it is so important to them, but fortunately no one seems to remember who they were, nor should they.

Maybe it is now the time for today's fly fishers to pause and reflect for a short time on how our sport has evolved so far and where it stands today and how we all might like to see it progress in the future as we rush rapidly onward through the 21st century.

Little wonder it is only the 'Grumpy Old Men' of fly fishing today, who believe that the 'J.R. Hartley' syndrome is still alive and well, albeit on some quiet backwaters of this land, and that it has still a great deal to commend it even in 2009. Wouldn't it be interesting to hear what the redoubtable 'J.R.' himself would have to say on the subject!

CHAPTER 20

DRESSED TO IMPRESS OR DRESSED TO KILL: MINIMALIST TACKLE REQUIREMENTS FOR FLY FISHING

Like many fly fishermen before me, as and when I progressed from my first introduction with the help of my father into this fascinating sport of fly fishing, my stock of artificial flies has increased sequentially over the years. My collection not only grew in numbers, but also in the diversity of patterns, whether devised and tied by myself or purchased at the local tackle shop. Maybe it is through nostalgia, but no matter how tatty some of these flies have become over the years, either by use or just age, I still find it hard to weed them out and consign the rubbish to the dustbin. Therefore, I have many redundant fly boxes crammed full of flies that I now rarely open, let alone take to the river.

The same applies to the rest of my fly fishing tackle. Of the many trout rods I have accumulated over the years, I find that I now regularly use only two of them. One for dry fly fishing and the other for the heavier duties for still water trout or sea trout. The rest gather dust under the stairs where there are split cane rods, glass fibre rods and more modern yet early models of carbon fibre, all of which were deemed to be state of the art at their time of acquisition. Throughout my fishing life I have had a love for cane rods, because not only was split cane the only material used for fly rod making when I started fly fishing, but it is the love and respect one develops for a split cane rod. Each rod is an individual work of art that has been delicately and lovingly handcrafted by a dedicated skilful craftsman using split cane which is a natural material. For many like myself, this has been for me a joyous lifelong love affair with split cane rods, the physical beauties and seductive charms of which have captivated me all my fishing life. This is a feeling only a true fly fisherman can even begin to explain, particularly if one is predominantly a dry fly fisher who caught his first wild trout on a split cane fly rod.

It is either through laziness or experience drawn from 50 years of dry fly fishing that has taught me that to be comfortable when fly fishing is paramount. Equally important is the selection of suitable colours and shades of the clothing worn. Having decided upon the right clothes to wear, the next thing for me is to ensure I carry as little equipment as possible. I cannot help but smile privately to myself when I observe some of today's so-called chalk stream 'experts' fly fishing. Not only are they usually weighed down with a mass of useless equipment dangling from every corner of their clothing, but also some demonstrate a naive immunity or a decided lack of understanding as to the colour and shades of the clothing they should wear whilst fly fishing, particularly for wild trout in a chalk stream. I have seen some of the best casting instructors in the world fishing – their casting abilities may be excellent, but that alone does not make a successful fish catcher! Being a good caster alone is no substitute for knowledgeable adept stream craft. Ideally a combination of both skills is required, plus being able to think like a trout and then think like a patient hunter who has not eaten for a week!

These important aspects of fly fishing I learnt in my early formative years when I had the great privilege and opportunities as a young river keeper to observe, listen and learn and say nothing whilst sat at the feet of my father and those legends of fly fishing, Frank Sawyer, Dermot Wilson and 'Ollie' Kite. Not only observing the demonstrations of their streamside field craft when stalking rising trout, but also mentally noting the way they were dressed as they entered into the stalk. The success rate of any hunter relies so much on adept field craft in the matter of the approach and the skilful ability to merge body outline discreetly into the natural surrounding environment, thus enabling the fisher to get closer to his prey to deliver the delivery cast. Today I believe so many fly fishers reduce their chances of deceiving a fish when they dress in these modern bright-coloured shirts, gaudy baseball caps and multi-pocketed waistcoats which are also made of bright shades of coloured materials. When on a river bank and dressed in such garb, these fishermen stand out like an on-duty motorway policeman, as any slightest movement they make can be readily picked up a mile away. Is it any wonder any self-respecting trout in their vicinity retires rapidly from the scene?

In fact, to further illustrate this very point, I remember so well a remark made on one occasion by 'Ollie' Kite himself. We were sat together one lunchtime outside of the fishing hut sharing a glass or two of his famous homemade rocket fuel that he euphemistically called dandelion and burdock wine! He said that it was not until he had recently watched some film footage of himself fly fishing for trout, did he realise that the shirt he was wearing in the film made him stand out like a sore thumb on the river bank. Being one of his army shirts, it was originally a standard army issue khaki colour which, when new, blended well into the general background, but after years of wear he had not noticed or realised that with the constant wear, washing and ironing, the original colour and shade had been bleached out and it had now taken on a very light beige/cream colour which stood out quite vividly, even on black and white film.

Today's trout fisher's brightly coloured uniform has, or is now, almost become a standard twenty-first century game angling dress code and this is aptly illustrated on some of the glossy covers and in pages of game fishing magazines. Before being taken to task, I would admit that in days gone by even those doyens of fly fishing of yesteryear, such as those mentioned above, also conformed to a certain current dress code that was regarded as standard required fishing kit at the time. However, in those days it was one of sober neutral-coloured shirts and pullovers, tweed hats, and tweed jackets over topped with waxed Barbour jackets if it was wet, and brown or dark green corduroy trousers stuffed into wellies or thigh boots. In my earliest days on the Itchen, neck ties were expected to be worn by all fishermen, including the keeper if he was going to act as ghillie for the day! Thank goodness the strict adherence to this rigid dress code was relaxed with the advent of the swinging sixties! However, the major difference between those days and today was that for yesterday's anglers, whatever style of clothes they were dressed in, the unwritten rule was that the clothes worn were to be of a universal colour mixture of dull green, olive and brown, all of which readily merged into the natural background colours and shades of the riverside environment.

One has only to ask any expert pigeon shooter or game keeper what his killing success rate would be if he wore one of today's brightly coloured baseball hats and shirt when sat in a pigeon hide expecting to attract wary wild wood pigeons into his decoys! His obvious answer surely would apply equally to anyone stalking wild trout in a river if dressed in the same bright colours. So often I see on the chalk streams in particular, anglers dressed in outrageous colours just because today's fashions appear to decree that in game angling, the clothing now worn in the UK has become so orientated towards all that is popular on the American scene. It appears to be today's fashion to wear and be seen to be wearing these bright-coloured garments. Although many were originally designed in the USA, much of this type of clothing is now made in China! Dressing in lightweight, ventilated, cool fabrics of a vibrant colour is no doubt very comfortable in hot weather when worn for attending the CLA Game Fair and fishing shows around the country or for attracting attention while delivering casting demonstrations. They may also be fine for the sweltering heat and bright tropical sunlight when wading the bone fish flats of Belize or tarpon fishing from a boat off Key West, for which use I suggest these clothes were originally designed. However, I am not quite sure these bright colours are conducive to, or were designed for, successful stalking of wild trout in a traditional UK trout river.

However, on a completely different tack, I must mention wading in chalk streams. I agree implicitly with the accepted upstream chalk stream approach, that fly fishers should at all times commence fishing at the very bottom boundary of their allotted beat and work upstream. Working up a chalk stream in this manner with a fly rod is one of Halford's doctrines that will probably stand the test of time! In my experience on the River Itchen, due to the nature of the soft riverbed of the Itchen, any form of wading can readily put into suspension a great deal of silt and can often loosen quantities of aquatic weed, blanket weed, and algae – the effects of which will most certainly detract from the quality of the sport of any angler who is fishing directly downstream. 'No wading' regulations, for this very reason, are therefore common on many of the beats on the chalk streams. These arbitrary rules are made and upheld solely for the benefit of the fisherman.

Being confined to fish from the river bank only, may well test and challenge the casting skills of the fly fisher to cover some rising trout, and it will invariably increase the incidence of drag. However, that all adds to the beauty and charms of the chalk stream challenge. However, a blind eye is usually turned by the river keeper for the odd one leg in the water that enables a cast to be made to a trout that is tight in under the bank and there is dense overhanging vegetation along the river bank. I have over the years often experienced sudden changes in the clarity in the River Itchen for no apparent reason, which immediately puts down any trout feeding off the surface.

On investigation I have found the cause of the coloured water usually to be just one angler a mile or more upstream wading to and fro and up the middle of his beat. Even such an apparently innocent and minor in-stream disturbance can and does affect fishing for long distances downstream. Before someone puts pen to paper, I suggest with today's increased fishing pressure, if wading was allowed on every beat of the chalk streams we would immediately lose one of the main characteristics that the chalk streams are noted for... gin-clear water!

Returning to tackle requirements, nowadays whenever I fish my home chalk stream, or in fact any river that holds trout, I now make sure to fish with the absolute minimum amount of tackle according to the conditions of the day. In fact, I have refined my tackle requirements down to absolute basics. Other than the rod, reel and line, all my requirements for a day's dry fly trout fishing, or come to that for the entire season, can be stowed quite easily in the two breast pockets of my dark green fishing shirt and one trouser pocket.

So often I have seen anglers fishing up a chalk stream and carrying with them two or three rods made up, ranging sometimes from a one weight through to maybe a six weight! Many now even wear chest waders when they are not necessary, plus the obligatory bulging multi-pocketed waistcoat over which is worn a waist bag and even a knapsack on the back, all of which are crammed full of items and gadgets, many of which I am sure have not seen the light of day for years, and when viewed from a distance these figures resemble a cross between on overladen mountain yak and an over-decorated Christmas tree. All topped off with a host of extra items of kit that cannot be stored in the waistcoat because all forty-eight pockets are already so full, so they suspend all this extra tinsel from every conceivable corner of their clothing.

OK, maybe all this kit is required and has its uses if the angler has hiked over twenty miles up to some isolated highland loch and intends to camp out for a week or has trekked for days up many miles of a wilderness river system in New Zealand. However, is it really necessary to carry all this gear when actually fly fishing on our more popular trout rivers in the UK?

OK, cynical I may now be in the springtime of my senility, but I have learnt to say nothing and merely smile inwardly to myself, as I am so often brought down to earth after catching sight of my own reflection in a car window... so, who am I to make any sartorial comment?

For interest, my minimalist dry fly and nymph trout fishing kit would consist of the following basic items:

- Sage 9ft 5wt SLT 590-4 (four piece)
- A thirty-year-old Hardy 'Lightweight' Reel loaded with a Snowbee DT 5wt floater with a 13 ft. tapered Umpqua leader attached
- A spare Umpqua 13ft tapered leader down to 7x
- A 25 metre spool of tippet material 7x
- A 25 metre spool of tippet material 5x
- A small cheap clear plastic six-sectioned dry fly box for my selection of flies and nymphs; Capacity of which circa 100 assorted dry flies, emergers and nymphs
- A small 10 gm plastic container of 'Abolene' which is my preferred floatant
- Lastly for a priest I use my trusty twenty-year-old Swiss Army 'Anglers' knife, which is the complete fisherman's tool box with scissors and a disgorger plus all the other tools, including tweezers,

can opener and obligatory cork screw, which rests in my left-hand
trouser pocket, attached to my belt by a stout cord.

I wear an aged baggy 1920s-style brown tweed cap that has a good peak,
and although I hate baseball caps and wouldn't be seen dead in one I do
have to admit their long peaks are useful in bright conditions.

Besides wearing wellies or thigh waders for kneeling and bank crawling
when it's wet, I may also carry a lightweight hooded nylon waterproof if
rain threatens, which doubles up as a small groundsheet if the banks are
wet and a sit-down fag break rest is needed, and after use can be folded
away to nothing and stuffed easily into the back trouser pocket like a pair
of golfing gloves. I am more than happy to use this basic selection of kit
wherever and whenever I fish for trout in the UK, be it moving water
or still water. If it happens to be cold, then I wear a suitable
olive-coloured fleece.

With this kit neatly stowed about my body, there is still plenty of room
left for my fags, lighter, handkerchief, an odd bar of chocolate and even,
heaven forbid, my mobile phone! Complete comfort and freedom of
movement is the object, as I do detest to be constrained and cluttered up
by any excess equipment around my body.

A good pair of Polaroid glasses are obligatory but as for a landing net?
No, I prefer not to use one and will only under protest take a small folding
one which is clipped to my belt or slung around my back when fishing a
river that has high banks when played out fish cannot be drawn safely into
the hand for release or despatch. I find landing nets have a great affinity
for attaching themselves to every passing bramble, barbed wire fence,
or stile, and when required are nowhere to be found but usually turn up
some time later skulking in the long grass a hundred yards down the
river bank!

Probably few will agree with my philosophies or even with my
selection of kit, but they both suit me in the way I wish and enjoy to fly

fish, and I have the utmost respect for those who may not agree or wish to differ. I am certainly not competitive when it comes to fishing and although I enjoy deceiving trout and possibly would catch more of them if I did become more competitive with other anglers, to me inter angler competition is not the aim of the game in my book. Fly fishing to me is a solitary form of enjoyment and if indeed there is any competition in fly fishing, the challenge comes from dealing with the conditions that nature sets before me, and as for competition – that is just between me and that elusive trout over there!

Although I have caught my fair share of fish over the years, some of my most memorable days spent fly fishing have been blank when it comes to numbers of trout caught. Spending many wonderful days in some of the most beautiful wild natural surroundings on Earth, where my attention has been captivated for every minute of the day with the most beautiful and stunning scenery around me and in observing some of the most incredible native flora and fauna, has been one of the greatest pleasures in my fly fishing life... I have been very fortunate over the years, mainly through my work as a river keeper and a trout habitat consultant, to have had the opportunity to experience many such wonderful fishless days, not only on my home chalk streams of Hampshire but on some remote highland burns and lochs of Scotland and in the 'big sky' wildernesses of Montana, Wyoming and the rugged wilds of Northern Ontario, Labrador, New Brunswick and Quebec. I have been very privileged to visit and experience and appreciate the natural beauties of these wonderful wild places and consign my private records of them to the memory banks of my mind for instant recall in my later years... all just because I am a fly fisherman!

CHAPTER 21
ITCHEN MEMORIES OF CATCH AND RELEASE

The river keeper, having spotted the serious bend in the delicate cane rod from some distance away, instinctively knew that the angler had risen and hooked a good-sized wild brown Itchen trout. From the spot on the river bank where the angler was knelt playing the fish, the keeper also had a good idea which fish he had on, as he knew his river and resident fish so well that only one particular good trout could be caught from that spot. Knowing the angler well, the keeper appreciated also that he would wish to be left on his own to play and net this good fish. After a few tense minutes of give and take, the trout was gently drawn over the waiting net and the angler stepped into the river and slipped his hand down the leader and gently plucked the barbless iron blue dun dry fly from the jaws of the trout. The angler had laid his rod down on the river bank and was kneeling in the water gently cradling the trout, head upstream in the cool current, by the time the keeper arrived. Together and in total silence, they both admired the handsome black and red spotted perfectly proportioned wild brown trout as it recovered its strength in the gentle hands of the angler. "Would you like me to weigh the fish? I have a very accurate set of pocket scales, so we can slip the fish back into the net and weigh both together before we return the fish unharmed," the keeper asked.

The angler did not raise his head but slowly shook it from side to side.

"I have a tape measure in my pocket. Would you like me to measure it?" volunteered the keeper, knowing that American anglers usually measured their fish rather than weigh them.

Again, the angler did not even look up or raise his head but merely slowly shook it from side to side.

"Would you like me to take a photograph of it for you? As I have my digital camera with me, it won't take a second and you can then e-mail it to your friends back home," the keeper enquired.

Again, the slow shake of the head, and the trout – now sufficiently recovered – with one powerful bound, darted off into the depths of the cold River Itchen. The angler watched the disappearing trout and, slowly straightening up, turned, and speaking for the first time, explained to the keeper in a slow soft southern drawl.

"Thank you for your suggestions, but I have this vivid picture in my mind of how big that fish is and I'll carry that with me throughout the year and during the hot, humid days of summer when I am working in New York. I'll remember this beautiful green valley, this wonderful river and this very spot on it, the gentle breeze that carries the smell of the new mown bank grass, and the sigh of those willows behind us, this pale blue Hampshire sky above us, and the swallows taking flight off the surface of the river, and most of all (pointing into the river), I'll remember that fish. I don't want this wonderful clear mental picture I have cluttered up with any statistics of weight and length or even a photograph, as none would ever compare with the one I carry up here," said the angler, as he tapped the side of his head.

As the keeper wended his way up the river bank alone, head bowed in deep contemplation, he became very aware that there are some priceless angling memories that money can never buy.

CHAPTER 22

PROBLEMS WITH INTRODUCED SPECIES

During my lifetime spent as a river keeper, much of that time has been spent identifying and becoming familiar with many of the various species of flora and fauna that inhabit the rivers and river valleys. This occupation becomes second nature to a river keeper. Few species in nature do not have their allotted place within the big picture of life. However, at times, some creatures and plants and insects find their way into places where nature did not originally intend them to be. This situation usually occurs when man is involved; when he intentionally moves creatures or plants from one place to another. However, nature itself decides at times to encourage the movement of these creatures from one habitat to another. Any new plant, animal or insect arrival, be it introduced by man or as a natural arrival that has not been recorded before in Great Britain, is immediately identified as an alien species by the scientists. Despite not being trained as a scientist in this sphere of natural history, I do however have to take to task some scientists who appear to me to suffer from tunnel vision when identifying and discussing the merits of some species of the flora and fauna of Great Britain as being designated indigenous or alien.

When does an introduced species become eligible to be called wild? What indeed are the differences between 'introduced' and 'indigenous', 'wild' and 'native'? When does 'introduced' become 'indigenous' and 'wild' become 'native'?

As ever, I have no wish to enter into the ongoing debate on the genetic integrity of brown trout (*Salmo trutta*) which are a species of fish common to many rivers and waters of Great Britain and have certainly been evident in these waters since the retreat of the last ice age. However, man in his wisdom has over the centuries exploited this species to his advantage by capturing mature native brood stock and rearing their offspring in enclosed waters and used the resulting captive offspring to eat or seed back into rivers and lakes for aesthetic, biological, and/or commercial fishing reasons. Now the 64,000-dollar question is what are the differences, if any, between these artificially reared fish and the native fish that are still abundant in our waters? Although a fish has been reared by the hand of man, is it any different to its native brothers and sisters? I believe not, although I accept on release its behaviour patterns may be somewhat different to its native brothers and sisters and that it may not even adapt or survive very well in the wild environment due mainly to the nature of its upbringing in unnatural surroundings and being fed artificially. However, if it does survive after release to breed naturally with a released compatriot or with a native cousin, the resulting offspring will not be radically different in any way to the offspring of a natural native pairing. The offspring of a pairing of stocked fish reared in captivity and then released to breed naturally can still legitimately be described as genuine wild trout. These offspring cannot be termed native as humans have interfered with its breeding albeit in a previous generation. It is suggested also, that with the modern genetic knowledge available today, that any genetic comparisons made between these 'wild trout' and the resident 'natives' would indicate that little significant genetic change will have taken place due to man's interference. From the time of release, for the subsequent offspring of these introduced fish, Darwin's theory of survival of the fittest kicks in along with the fish's capacity to adapt successfully to the ecological conditions of the water in which it is born.

Experiences noted from some older generations of chalk stream angler indicate that there were noticeable physical differences between compared examples of native River Test trout, native Itchen trout and native Kennet trout. I remember well in the 1960s catching a traditional 'green back' brown trout on the Kennet and comparing it with a native trout from the upper Itchen. Yes, there were noticeable physical differences. The shape and colour and markings of brown trout differ markedly when comparisons are made between the many discrete populations that live in so many differing and diverse ecological conditions throughout the British Isles. This comes about primarily through many uninterrupted generations of natural breeding of 'like with like' in isolated situations.

I would dispute strongly that native trout fight more vigorously than wild trout or that they are generally any more difficult to catch. Determining the fighting potential of a trout, or specific strain of trout, is usually more reliant on a combination of either water temperature and/ or quality, food availability, general habitat conditions and the cumulative stress levels within a fish at the time, than on the integrity of its breeding history or genetic makeup. However, there are in nature exceptions to the rule!

Unfortunately, many of the historical noted physical characteristics of some recognised strains of native brown trout experienced and observed by anglers years ago have now almost been completely lost as numerous annual introductions will have probably diluted many of these physical phenomena. If perchance a river system could return to a natural self-sustaining population of trout, no doubt over many generations of natural reproduction within the river these specific physical characteristics may well slowly reappear once more.

Returning to the original question of what is indigenous and what is introduced, I recall, quite vividly, discussing with a visiting angler, who happened to be a qualified botanist, the various wild flowers that were evident along the river margins. One particular species that was in its full flower at the time was the 'yellow musk', as we river keepers call it, yet identified by the expert as *Mimulus luteus*. This plant is abundant along the river margins of the Itchen at Martyr Worthy and has long been one of my favourite species of wild flower. This plant is common along the whole river system as it is on the neighbouring River Test and indeed on many rivers throughout Gt Britain and is even seen as far afield as the outer isles of Scotland.

Unfortunately, the expert botanist said, "Ah yes, but the *Mimulus leuteus* is not native to this country; it is an introduced species."

"Introduced by who and when?" I asked.

Unfortunately, that question the botanist was unable to answer! Since then, I understand that the earliest written records that mention 'yellow musk' appear in Edward Newman's botanical magazine *The Phytologist* in 1815!

The whole aspect of introduced species has since been of interest to me and I have made some interesting discoveries on the subject. One question that begs to be asked and should be asked and answered is "What is a British wild flower?"

Should not the same rule apply not only to plants but also to animals and insects, whether a species has been introduced accidentally or purposely imported by humans? Surely a plant or animal, once it thoroughly establishes itself in and on our soil or waters and demonstrates that it can establish and maintain a self-sustaining existence in the wild, then whatever the species, it should then be recognised as a resident British species. This is irrespective of it being deemed detrimental or beneficial to the general ecological health of the countryside, either aquatic or terrestrial.

If we think about it, the common rabbit has been here for 2000 years or more yet is still termed as an introduction! Why? Furthermore, if we look closer, we find many of our well-known species come into this category: the brown rat, the black beetle, the pheasant, capercailzie, the red-legged partridge, the fallow deer, and the garden snail, the stinging nettle and many more species of plant and animal life. All of which have arrived with or without man's help. Among the more recent horrors include the North American mink, grey squirrel, ruddy duck, Japanese mitten crab, Japanese knotweed and Himalayan balsam and giant hogweed, to name just a few that come to mind.

If we think about it, going back in time since the end of the last ice age, it can be said that every known species of plant, animal, or insect in Great Britain has at some time either been introduced by man or has, via natural means, brought itself into this country from elsewhere. Has any species we see today been resident in Great Britain since the dawn of time? I do not think so. It is just that some species arrived here before others. This is an ongoing process which at times has been aided and abetted by man and is a situation which will continue well into the future, no doubt.

In my experience, observing the way a new species, whether introduced or not, adapts to the ecosystem and finds its niche in the web of life and prospers has taught me a great deal about some species. For example, when the grayling was introduced by man into the upper River Itchen in the mid-1980s, the numbers initially exploded for several years and it seemed that the river was packed with grayling and no other species. In fact, the excessive numbers of grayling ruined the dry fly fishing for wild trout for several seasons and still does in places. However, as time passed, like it or not the grayling slowly adapted to the conditions by making room for itself within the ecosystem, and now they have established a natural self-sustaining population that is within the balance of fish biomass within the river. Although, it must be said that the presence of the grayling has significantly reduced the productivity of the native brown trout. Something had to give to allow for these new species of fish to proliferate.

The introduction of an alien species, as the grayling is, to the upper Itchen where grayling have never existed before has, as predicted at the time, now seen to have had detrimental effects on the river and on the traditional angling experiences for wild brown trout that the upper Itchen has been noted for throughout the past two hundred years. Having said that, it is at this stage however, like it or not, the grayling population of the upper Itchen should now be identified biologically as a self-sustaining wild species of fish, because that is what they have unfortunately become. The foolhardiness of these artificial introductions should stand as a prime irreversible example of what not to do regarding introductions of alien species into any aquatic ecosystem. Similarly, this principle should apply to all alien plants, animals, and insects, etc. I find it sad that some angling organisations and scientists condone, and even welcome, the introduction of alien species into our rivers, e.g. grayling into the upper Itchen, when the river owners, fishery managers and keepers rightly treat any alien introductions with total disdain and try to eliminate them. Many species have been introduced over the centuries into this country and this will continue to be the case, but it is surely biological folly to actively promote and condone their proliferation.

Let us therefore strive to do more to protect and enhance what we have left of the natural environment of the UK for all the flora and fauna that nature supplies, and let nature alone determine and select what species within it thrives the best. Trying to reintroduce creatures that were historically once prolific within the UK into today's natural environment which has been dramatically altered over the centuries is, in my opinion, unproductive and a waste of time and money. Protect and enhance what natural environment we have left but allow nature to decide which wild creatures make it their home. Over-simplistic this concept may be, but once the concept of holistic river catchment management is adopted, whereby within the aquatic ecosystem everything is interconnected, then these simple principles become more applicable.

CHAPTER 23

RAINBOW TROUT BEHAVIOUR

In response to recent correspondence received on the behaviour of today's stocked rainbows, I can only call upon my own experiences in the rearing of brown trout in stew ponds for subsequent stocking out into still waters and rivers. Albeit my work was with brown trout for stocking the lower beats of the Itchen and Test, yet I believe the principles discussed here would apply equally to rainbows.

It is suggested that since the introduction from the West Coast of the USA of the two recognised separate strains of 'rainbows' into this country back in the middle 1800s, the stocks of 'generic rainbows' that are now available from commercial hatcheries in the UK consist of a mixture of these two strains. The present genetic makeup of what are now called 'rainbows' now consists of a mixture of the landlocked traits of the Mt Shasta or Kamloops strain and the anadromous steelhead strain, both of which were introduced into this country around the same time. These two varieties of rainbow have now been so intermixed that now we have just the one generic 'rainbow' which is now recognised as a species and has been now reclassified as *Oncorhnchus mykiss* from *Salmo gairdneri*.

Hatchery managers have over the years been very wary of introducing fresh blood into their hatcheries for fear of introducing diseases and rightly so. This has inevitably created closed hatchery strains of rainbows that have been inadvertently selected for good growth over the years by the hatchery manager. These fish have over many generations adapted to their locality with brood stocks selected from within the close confines of these populations, which produce trout that survive and grow well in these intensive stew pond conditions. Little thought, however, seems to be given to how these trout behave when released as stock fish!

I believe it may take many generations of artificial trout rearing to alter the actual genetic fingerprint of a strain of fish. So, after 100 years or more of intensive rearing, the actual genetic makeup of a species may not be altered all that much despite intensive inter-breeding. Therefore, the natural traits that we observed in the early generations of rainbow trout are still latent within today's generations. So, what has happened to change their observed feeding habits and behaviour patterns once these trout have been released into our rivers and still waters? As with most animals, including humans, the behaviour patterns and habits of young adults reflects the manner in which he or she was brought up during the formative years of their upbringing. So, the same principles apply, in my opinion, to trout reared in stew ponds, be they brown or rainbow.

From experience, I am now of the opinion that fish, and rainbow trout in particular, can in hatchery conditions be trained to hunt for food and be manipulated to feed in different ways. It is the changes in the manner that stocked rainbows feed and hunt for food once released into our fisheries, and in the manner they act and fight when hooked, that seems to concern many of today's more discerning anglers.

In the early days of the commercial manufacture of high-protein trout foods, except for the swim up fry and par stages when fine granulated food was fed, most stew-bred trout from these life stages onwards were fed on floating pellets. These floating pellets were very expensive to produce and as the cost of the protein content of these pellets in the form of White Sea fish meal also increased, commercial trout producers demanded a cheaper form of food. So, the slow-sinking and fast-sinking pellet was devised which still contained the high protein levels needed for growth but now were not required to float. It is far cheaper to produce denser sinking pellets than the floating variety which are very expensive to manufacture, as it requires extra heating and moulding processes to cook and shape each pellet to make them float.

The denser the pellet the cheaper it is to produce and the quicker it sinks to the bottom of the stew pond. It was soon noticed that trout would readily learn to stand on their heads and peck up these sunken pellets off the floor of the stew pond, just like tench or carp sifting muddy gravel at the bottom of a natural pond. Fast-sinking extruded pellets were therefore found to be the most economical food form for producing fast-growing trout.

I suggest that feeding sinking pellets has been common practice for many years in most commercial hatcheries. Therefore, the many generations of rainbows that now have been produced have been continually trained during their lives in the hatchery to seek food on the floor or to take fast-sinking food on its way to the floor of the rearing pond. These stew-bred rainbows have not had the chance in their entire lives to learn to seek and find and take food from or near the surface of the water. They have for many generations adapted to only looking down to seek food! It has been shown quite conclusively that trout can be taught to feed in certain ways and once learnt they do not forget even if feeding methods are changed.

However, even if certain rearing regimes can be shown to have significant effects on the subsequent behaviour of released rainbows, then serious consideration should be given to other hatchery practices. One that could have even more significant effects on the post-release behaviour of rainbows is the increasing practice of rearing and releasing triploid rainbow trout into fisheries. For the fishery manager the whole principle of rearing and using these trout is quite understandable economically, as these fish are virtually 100% sexless and so do not sexually mature. This obviates many problems that fishery managers have had to contend with over the years. When natural trout were used, anglers would complain at certain times of the year of catching egg-bound females and ugly black males streaming with milt. Despite this, plus in their favour, I sincerely believe that triploid rainbows are far more benign in their behaviour after release than the old-fashioned rainbow trout. So, as a species, the now 'generic rainbow' trout has undergone many changes since it was first introduced as two unblemished natural wild varieties of game fish all those years ago. So, it is of little wonder that the behaviour patterns of today's very 'mixed up' rainbow trout has altered somewhat. The EA and the Game Conservancy together are undergoing researches into the pros and cons of triploid in brown trout, so it will be very interesting to see what their findings are and whether their findings can be applied to rainbows. There is little doubt in my mind that hatchery-reared rainbow behaviour has changed significantly over the years. Rarely these days do hooked rainbows regularly tail walk or spend more time in the air than in the water or make long runs out to the backing when being played, as did the rainbows of twenty to forty or more years ago.

If asked what could be done to improve the angling qualities of stocked rainbows, I would suggest that fresh new genuine wild blood from natural wild resources could be introduced back into our rainbow hatcheries to perk up the dull resident stocks. Thoughtful game keepers regularly introduce new strains of cock birds or hens to their resident pheasant stock. The principle objective being to maintain and improve the quality and diversity of their resident stocks.

With hatchery trout, feeding with floating pellets may help to train stock trout to at least look up in the world, not down! New or different rearing regimes could be considered that include reducing stocking intensities in rearing ponds. The objectives should be to produce fitter stock fish and get away from the soft flabby fish that have been ad-lib fed in sluggish water in stew ponds that have little throughput of water. To produce top-quality stock trout that perform well when released, experience teaches that they should be reared in suitable densities in quite fast-moving water and fed on floating food. These conditions have been shown to produce fit, lean, hard-fleshed stock trout that show greater sporting qualities when released than trout that are overfed on sinking food, fins damaged by being raised in overcrowded ponds in sluggish water. Finally, until proven otherwise, we have to question the effects or benefits of using rainbow triploids against introducing more natural rainbow diploids from a reputable disease-free source.

As for angling methods, I believe that anglers have over the years by observation and fishing experience, adapted and developed their methods to cope with the changing habits and characteristics of today's stocked rainbow trout. One thing is for sure, the fighting qualities of today's rainbows are not a patch on the trout I used to catch (occasionally!) in my youth some 50 years ago!

CHAPTER 24

"THE TIMES THEY ARE A CHANGIN'"

Now well into the springtime of my senility, there is now more time to reflect with others of a similar age and disposition on a lifetime of fly fishing. Without exception, whenever fly fishing is discussed within these circles there is agreement that our beloved sport of fly fishing has witnessed many changes throughout our fishing years. Changes, some good and some of which may not have all been for the betterment of our sport. There is, as in nature, nothing more constant than change and the sport of fly fishing is no exception to this rule.

Changes for the good are welcome; however, changes for the worse should be challenged by all who really care for our sport. The problem is, however, who other than the individual can arbitrate on what is good and what is not? One thing is for certain and that is fly fishing has progressed through the years and has developed exponentially with the regular introduction and use of modern manufacturing technology and new materials.

The often-quoted timeworn clichés, "The fishing is not as good as it was when I was a boy" and "There is more to fly fishing than just catching fish", still echo around our fisheries today. Experience also teaches today's 'Grumpy Old Men' of fly fishing that the fly fishing of 2005 is now somewhat different when compared to fly fishing as they knew it in 1955. The greatest changes have been in the innovations within the tackle scene, aided by the introduction and use of new space age materials and improved technology in manufacture. Whether all the observed changes that these improvements have spawned have all been for the good is open for debate. There appear to be signs that the historic attitudes and ethics within angling, and fly fishing in particular, have changed or are coming under threat. Or is it, maybe, that fly fishing has been inevitably led to change since those halcyon days of pre-1955 and that these changes are due to environmental influences beyond our control? Whatever it may be, there is a growing realisation, particularly within the ranks of the older generation, that fly fishing as they knew it in their younger days has lost – or is in danger of losing – contact with its historic traditions, sporting ethics and philosophies that have been handed down from generation to generation. On the other hand, even today's older generation are not advocating returning to the rigid, tunnel vision, dogmatic Halfordian attitudes that shackled fly fishing in bygone years.

It has, in many cases, been the traditions and sporting ethics set down in the writings of the recognised influential doyens of the early days of fly fishing that have influenced and attracted so many people into a lifelong love of our sport, once they had been introduced to its beauties and complexities. This wonderful sport of ours has, through absorbing its rich literature and in practical participation with a rod in hand, afforded so many thought-provoking natural challenges, endless enjoyment, relaxation and satisfaction to so many anglers. It has been that way for many generations of fly fishers in particular, and most of all it has greatly enriched so many human lives along the way.

The great technical advances in modern tackle design and manufacture has encouraged the development and use of some new and very ingenious methods for catching game fish, some of which it is feared now bear little resemblance to fly fishing as it was known in 1955! As these new methods have evolved and are developed and used under the heading of fly fishing, then it is surely for the angler himself to voluntarily impose upon himself any arbitrary regulations he sees fit that maintains their sporting uses. The criteria for setting these arbitrary conditions should be to maintain a good code of sporting practice that respects the prey and contributes to the maintenance of the written and unwritten but voluntarily accepted ethics and sporting traditions of the art of fly fishing.

Experience teaches that heavy overstocking with outsized fish, and associated fixed bag limits, can at times encourage a human affliction called 'limititis'. So it is little wonder many fishermen tire of such regular predictable angling experiences and some either give up fly fishing altogether or, as their skills improve, move on to seek further challenges to their fly fishing skills by hunting other genuine wild species of fish, either in the sea or freshwater. It does not take much time for the true fly fisherman to appreciate the challenges that nature offers and that the measure of the quality of the fishing experience and the natural beauty of the surroundings within fly fishing is inversely proportional to its artificiality.

Unfortunately, the sight and sound of a rising wild trout is now fast becoming a rare experience on many waters, as the incidence of natural insect life continues to dwindle. So, could it be the lack of fly life that is responsible for stimulating some of the observed changes in fly fishing attitudes and the methods now employed by some anglers, which in turn may be indirectly compromising our sport's historic traditions and ethics? Changes that now see people fishing the hallowed dry fly chalk stream beats for trout downstream and across with weighted lures, because there is little or no active fly life these days to bring trout up to the surface to feed.

New tactics have evolved to catch trout and grayling that include the use of a fly rod for an array of 'touch ledgering' techniques that entail using 'sacrificial' heavy weighted hookless 'nymphs' (lead shot) below a 'washing line' of droppers with a 'bite indicator' (float) attached to the leader. These fishing methods are quite legal and there is little doubt at times these methods are very successful at fish catching, but can these methods really be classified under the heading of fly fishing? Where can a line be drawn or, in fact, and more importantly, should such a line be drawn?

There appears to be a decided ever-widening grey area developing between true fly fishing for game fish with a fly rod and some of the coarse fishing methods being developed and used with a fly rod. This being the case, should fly fishermen even care? Just as the 'upstream dry fly only to a rising fish' code of practice developed a hundred years or so ago, then similar arbitrary decisions will need to be made by fishery managers, fishery owners and the fly fisherman of today. The question is who determines if, how, when and where the use of these modern techniques are acceptable or not. Unfortunately, this dilemma has been bubbling away under the surface of game fishing for some considerable time and to date no one appears to be willing to come out and take a definitive position one way or the other. Not until a full and open discussion is embarked upon within game angling can any arbitrary decisions be considered to be adopted by individual fishery managers and anglers as to where the use of some of these increasingly controversial methods actually stand in today's broad-spectrum sport of game fishing. As the use of worms and prawns and shrimps as baits in salmon fishing has been abandoned on many major river systems in the UK, so the use of some of these modern trout and grayling methods may also need to be reviewed for similar reasons.

It should not be forgotten the ever-increasing serious threat that the anti-angling brigade will have on our sport which must be of major concern to all denominations of anglers.

No matter how well the heavily stocked 'Put and Take' trout fishery who operate a 'Catch and Release' policy is managed, these highly artificial fisheries may well be the first targets for those who wish to see all forms of angling banned. Why? Because multiple C&R on stocked trout could well open up our sport to accusations by the 'anti's' that game anglers in such circumstances are just playing with trout by catching and releasing them time and time again. 'Put and Take' is ethically and biologically acceptable providing all trout that are caught for the first time are killed. All anglers and fishery managers should be aware of these threats and be prepared to address them.

Even if we take all this into consideration, have things really changed all that much during the last fifty years? It is a matter of personal choice whether a fly fisherman adopts or adapts to these modern changes. The most important thing is that today's fly fishers continue to happily fish in the manner that suits them and in doing so also maintains and protects the historic values and philosophies and guidelines upon which our wonderful sport has evolved. So where does all this leave us today?

Each generation throws up its fair share of 'Grumpy Old Men' just like myself, so this is not a new human trait from which the fly fishing world is immune. If our precious rights to pursue our sport are to survive unmolested into the future and our angling waters protected and well-maintained for the benefit and use by our children's children, then maybe a good start in this direction would be a movement away from today's well-publicised statistics-driven angling culture, where size, weight and numbers are paramount.

Would it not be refreshing to read more accounts in the angling media of the appreciation of the beauty of our natural surroundings, or the intricacies of fishery management and why and where we fish, and that being there is equally, if not more, important than boring us stiff with so many bland and mostly uninteresting 'when I', 'how to' and 'how many' features? Promoting serious debate would be a good start on the part of the editors. These changes may then encourage the younger generations of game anglers to be more involved in their sport and along the way appreciate more the beauties and the more sporting, challenging and relaxing nature of fly fishing. The younger generations of fly fishers have to be taught and educated to appreciate there is more to fishing than just catching fish. The angling media has this education aspect as part of its duty to perform to its readers, so it should promote these needs and the importance of restoring the aquatic environment where it has been wrecked by man's influences. All of which will be a monumental task to achieve in this modern day and age.

CHAPTER 25

THE COMMANDER'S LAST TROUT

The commander had just celebrated his 82nd birthday, and as it was a warm spring morning, he decided to go fishing on his own rented beat of the upper River Itchen. He had fished the river for over 60 years and knew almost every flint of the riverbed and every inch of the river bank. The pressures of business and wartime service had taken their toll on his health and he now had difficulty in moving about; his vision was failing and even on this perfect spring morning his breathing was laboured.

The river keeper welcomed him to the river and assembled the classic 9ft 6in Hardy 'Itchen' cane rod with which the commander had fished for the past two and half decades with deadly accuracy and at times devastating success as many a wild Itchen brown trout would testify if they could!

Some sixth sense told the keeper to accompany the commander on this morning, as it seemed clear that he should not really be alone on the river. So together they walked quietly down to the river bank, the keeper selecting the appropriate fly for that morning (a size 18 iron blue dun) as they went. This was to be a study in ghillying in the time-honoured way, as within seconds of arriving at the water's edge the keeper's keen eye spotted a good trout rising gently and taking the odd natural iron blue dun as they sailed down between two clumps of swaying *Ranunculus*. After dressing the fly, the keeper instructed the commander to aerialise

10 yards of line. Habits of 60 year's fly fishing are never lost and with all his disabilities, and on one knee, the old man soon was gently flexing the rod and the fly line sailed slowly to and fro forming perfect loops - to the keeper it was poetry in motion.

"Now, upstream ten yards and 6 feet out from the bank," instructed the keeper. "Now again, but this time two feet more to the right."

"That's perfect, let it come, he's coming up - yes!"

The commander instinctively lifted into the fish, and the reel screamed as the fat trout rushed off across the river shaking its head as it went in its bid for freedom. Somehow the tiny hook held and perhaps the old veteran trembled more from excitement than infirmity as the keeper helped him to his feet and after a good fight finally netted the fish.

As the two men stood quietly admiring the heavily spotted 2lb wild brown trout in the net, the commander said, "Put him back, that fish deserves to live."

The keeper knelt down and gently removed the fly and reverently held the fish, head upstream in the cool water. Within seconds, the fish recovered and darted off unharmed but a mite wiser, no doubt.

The commander squinted at the fly on the end of his line and asked, "What fly was it?"

"An iron blue dun size 18," said the keeper.

With that, the commander took out his scissors and snipped off the fly and hooked it into the lapel of his old tweed fishing jacket. Again, he squinted at the leader he held in his hand and asked, "What tippet did you put on?"

"6x, sir," came the reply.

Again, the old man snipped off the tippet and neatly rolled it up in tight loops and carefully placed it in his wallet. Then he slowly reeled all his line back onto the reel and turned to the keeper and said, "Ron, that will be my very last trout... ever... thank you."

Now, who can say how much that trout was worth?

THE ORIGIN OF THE SPECIES: CHALK STREAM RIVER KEEPER AD CIRCA 1600 – 2009

A personal overview of the evolution and development of the chalk stream river keeper and his work on the Southern chalk streams of England.

Some of the earliest mention of the employment of men as water keepers on the chalk stream rivers of Southern England can be found in the early medieval records of the estates of Hampshire, the owners of which worked the lands on the flood plains and surrounding chalk downlands of the River Test and River Itchen. Many of these landowners also owned the riparian and milling rights of the stretches of the river that happened to run through these properties.

It was not until the construction of the many water mills in the early Middle Ages that local farm workers were employed in any number as water keepers by the mill owners. The job description of a water keeper employed between 1600 and 1850 would have been to ensure the river flows were not impeded and to enhance the water flows to and through the water mills. Water keepers' work at that time did not include caring for fish or fishing but was solely to increase the efficiency and use of the water flowing down the river to provide sufficient power to drive a mill to fulfil its duty for grinding corn and/or sawing wood.

More specifically, the duties of these early water keepers would have been firstly to construct and maintain the banks of the manmade mill leats that created a sufficient head of water above a mill which when released would power the mills, and secondly to keep the river channels above and below a mill clear of the super abundant annual aquatic weed growths for which these chalk streams have always been noted. Controlling the volumes of weed within these leats enhanced the river flow speeds towards and through the mill race. Although there are accounts of water mills being built and used as far back as the Roman occupation of the South of England, it was not until the early 1600s that milling became more popular with the advent and growth of more intensive forms of agriculture. At the peak of the milling era, historic records indicate that on average there was one operative mill constructed per mile of river, both on the rivers Itchen and Test. Many of these historic mills can still be seen in situ today but few, if any, are operative, as most have now been modernised into expensive desirable waterside residences. Others have since been dismantled, but on close observation evidence of these old mills can still be seen today. Many generations of water keepers were employed during the milling era to maintain the river banks and water flows for these mills.

During the late 1700s and through the 1800s the agricultural regimes gradually changed within the chalk stream valleys, mainly due to the demise of the wool and lamb trade and the advent of the industrial revolution which attracted workers out of the rural environment and encouraged them to move into the burgeoning industrial cities with the promise of well-paid employment. With the gradual demise of the milling operations the chalk streams became less and less used as agricultural rivers. The main exception being in areas where the drowning system of irrigation of the adjacent flood meadows to enhance grass growth was still practiced. Many numbers of men were employed to operate this labour-intensive drowning system; these were called 'drowners' or 'meadsmen'. The last recorded flood meadow to be purposely drowned in the Itchen Valley was in 1947. A 'flood meadow' is a meadow that the farmer could flood at will to enhance the growth of grass, whereas a 'water meadow' is a meadow that only flooded naturally during annual high-water events.

It was not until the sport of fishing for trout and other species of fish that lived in these rivers became recognised and developed as a sporting pastime by the landed gentry that life along these rivers began to change once again. Despite all the adverse effects of man's damaging land use practices in the catchments of these rivers during the preceding centuries, as soon as they abated and nature was allowed to take over the rivers, a wonderful natural healing process began. As the rivers cleaned themselves and natural fish populations recovered, these rivers were at the same time increasingly being used for the sport of fishing. Fly fishing at this juncture had yet to be perfected and popularised. Many of the early anglers fished these rivers using many and various methods, and the use of baits and lures was common (the use of which would be frowned upon today by a river keeper!). The use of horse hair blow lines attached to very long poles, at the end of which a bare hook baited with live mayflies was attached, signalled the dawn of fly fishing. This form of blow line fishing became a very popular sport in the spring of the year on the Test and Itchen. In some areas of the chalk streams where mayfly hatches were prolific, almost every mature tree and bush was felled and cleared that grew beside or even near the river course. The purpose of which was to utilise the best effect of any wind that blew from any direction to aerialise the fisherman's blow line. Old art prints of circa late 1700s of the middle Test and middle Itchen do tend to corroborate this. Some pictures and prints of the main river channel of the Test depict anglers fishing with a blow line without a mature tree in sight, yet the background topography depicted is quite accurate!

As the sport of fishing became more popular and fly fishing methods developed with the landed gentry, so the owners of these rivers became more aware of the value of the particular waters they owned. With this realisation, owners soon began to protect their rivers and enhance their precious assets. Many owners were not able or willing to get their own hands wet and dirty, so local labour was usually employed to do the job.

So, it was the sons and grandsons of the previous generations of water keepers whose job was originally to look after the water for the mills, who now once more became involved in the maintenance of the rivers, but this time their work was primarily for the fish and the fishing. Thus, around the early to middle 1800s dawned the age of what has come to be known as the 'Chalk Stream River Keeper'.

It is appropriate at this point to clarify the differences between a 'water keeper', a 'river keeper' and a 'water bailiff' – a question that is frequently asked.

A WATER KEEPER

A water keeper was employed by mill owners in earlier times solely to maintain the river banks and river channels to enhance the operations of the many water-powered mills during the times when the rivers were used mainly for agricultural purposes.

A RIVER KEEPER

The private riparian owner of a stretch of river employs a river keeper to protect, maintain, manage and enhance the natural aquatic habitat in and around the river for the benefit of fish and for the fishing.

A WATER BAILIFF

A water bailiff is a person employed by a recognised authority, either local or national, to implement and uphold all the rules and regulations set down by these authorities, such as local bylaws and the Salmon and Freshwater Fishery Acts.

As the sport of fishing developed, so more river keepers were employed on the chalk streams, and so the duties of a river keeper and the methods he devised and used began to evolve. The duties of a full-time river keeper were naturally closely geared to the workings of nature and the annual cycle of the four seasons. As the seasons wax and wane, so the work of a river keeper changes with the seasons. With experience, a river keeper learns what work needs to be done for the good of the river and the fish and will understand that there are the right and wrong times of the year to do the work.

Except for one or two salmon fisheries on the lower waters of the Test and Itchen, in most of the chalk stream beats of Hampshire the brown trout were and are the main species of fish that the early river keeper looked after. A river keeper needs to be fully acquainted with the intricate complete life cycle of the brown trout. With this valuable knowledge he must be able to pinpoint and identify any natural or manmade limiting factors within the trout's natural life cycle that may be controlling the survival of trout in his beat of the river. He then must be able to address to the best of his ability those limiting factors.

It is interesting to look back and trace how the river keeper's year of work and the methods he uses evolved in those early years on our chalk streams.

It is suggested that early river keepers tended the rivers in a similar manner their predecessor water keepers did before them. It is the riparian owner who employs the river keeper, and it is the owner who designates the duties of the river keeper. For example, the owner may require the river banks to be improved and maintained and kept in good repair, so it was safe to walk along and fish in reasonable comfort. Other duties may entail the provision for footpaths to be opened up and maintained along river banks and through the dense sedge beds that usually surrounded a river, and these were to be maintained throughout the year. Trees and bushes and reed beds were to be kept under control. Boundary fences, footbridges and board walks had to be built and maintained over side streams and impassable wetland areas. The weed in the river would need to be regularly cut to prevent summer flooding. Regular weed cutting in the river would extend the length of the fishing season. If not cut regularly the vigorous weed growth would rapidly choke the river and so reduce fishing time, as the river would become unfishable after June due to uncut emergent weed. So, these designated duties of a river keeper marked the transition from water keeper into river keeper. One thing is for sure in those days as it is today: no two river beats are the same and no two river keeping remits are the same!

The tools of the trade of these early river keepers were, at best, minimal with the ubiquitous English corn cutters scythe being the main tool used. Vegetation would be regularly hand cut with a scythe along the river banks to create and keep open footpaths. Scrub and sedge would be cleared from intended footpaths with hand tools, and most importantly the scythe was used to cut the aquatic weed in the river. Even today the 'Turk' hand scythe in the right hands is still by far the most efficient tool for selectively cutting weed in the river. The innovative early river keepers would also devise and design tools for specific jobs around the river, so if a tool was not commercially available they would dash off to the local blacksmith and under supervision get him to forge a new tool to tackle a particular job on the river.

Many of these old tools are still used by some of today's river keepers. There is hardly a river keeper's shed that does not have an array of strange shaped blacksmith-forged implements, the uses of many of which have now been lost in the mists of time.

Even so, the five-tined drag and the four-tined drag are both very useful tools in and around the river and are still in use today to shift silt or remove hung up weed from bridge piles. The mud pan that was devised to remove accumulated silt banks was another useful tool, but its use has diminished since more modern river keeping theories and practices have come about. Bill hooks, rip hooks and long handled slashers, axes and crosscut saws, spades and forks and shovels - not forgetting the wheelbarrow to carry these tools about the river - are still very much part of a river keeper's toolkit even today. All these old tools were in everyday use by the river keeper long before the days of mechanisation when every task around the river was done by hand. It is hard to imagine how long it took a river keeper to hand scythe every yard of footpath around a fishery. During the growing season, every day the scythe would not be far away from the hands of a river keeper, because as soon as he had finished cutting the grass around the river banks and paths he would be in the river – up to his armpits at times – cutting the river weed. Regular cutting and maintaining the river bank paths along the chalk streams became accepted practice when deep wading in the river to fish became banned on most beats. This ban was introduced due to the detrimental effects that wading by fishermen was thought to have on the riverbed and by the disturbance silt wading had on the clarity of the water for downstream users. On many fisheries it was decreed that all fishing should be done from the river bank, so riverside footpaths now had to be maintained to allow reasonable access to and along the river bank. Following on from this, the verdant growths of bankside vegetation that formed the fringe along the wet margins of the river had also to be kept in check by judicious trimming to allow fishers to cast their fly lines.

Having arrived into the river keeping profession in the late 1960s myself, mechanisation then had been around in river work for some time. River bank paths were then being cut by motorised self-propelled crosscut Allen Scythes or Mayfields. Rotary cutters came a little later, and it was some time before many river keepers were issued with modern chainsaws, strimmers and powered crosscut hedge cutters.

Having been introduced to all the tools of the river keeper profession by my predecessor and their uses demonstrated and explained to me, I took myself off to meet and talk to other river keepers. The reason I visited many of these experienced men who had been working all their lives on the rivers was to find out how, what, why, and when they did what they did on their rivers. One thing that I soon came to realise was that no two river keepers did any one job in the exact same way; each had their own priorities on the work in question. Furthermore, each river keeper had a slightly different remit set by his employer - that is if he had a remit at all, of which many did not! Another aspect that soon become clear was that each river keeper thought that his methods were best and that his river was better kept than anyone else's! No changes there then!

As time went by I also realised why the chalk streams had gained the dubious reputation of being over-manicured. Furthermore, river keepers and their long-established practices have recently been accused from some quarters of being partly responsible for the demise in the abundance of the natural fly life in our rivers. That, however, is another story!

Coming back to the over-manicuring accusation, in mitigation I suggest that any fishery that has a river bank that is deemed to be over-manicured, the fish in that river are usually no easier to catch than a fish in a river with an untended river bank. In fact, it is suggested that fish are harder to catch from a manicured bank than from an untended bank, as the manicured bank would most probably be fished more often than the untended bank! It may be more comfortable to fish from a manicured bank but that manicured state is usually what the owner demands on his river, so the river keeper has to comply. I would agree that where bank paths are cut to a ridiculous width like twenty or more foot then it is excessive and unnecessary. Three feet wide is about right. Trimming the bank fringe with a hedge cutter to box-like proportions is, again, over the top. A well-keepered beat on a chalk stream should give the impression of a keepered wilderness where access is comfortable for fishers, yet fishers come away at the end of the day with the feeling they have enjoyed a natural wilderness experience.

The accusations of over-manicuring, I believe, stems back to the early sixties when mechanisation came in with a rush which allowed river keepers to easily cut and maintain much larger areas of the ground in a far shorter period of time. In many instances river keepers did, in fact, overdo this day-to-day work, as it now took with modern tools a few hours to finish the job with a machine that once took weeks to finish by hand. With ease an extra swath or two could be cut, so bank paths soon became over-widened and many were cut so regularly that they looked like bowling greens, and the fringes along the river margins were trimmed with mechanical hedge cutters to simulate box hedges in a formal topiary garden. Some beats did become - and unfortunately some still are - severely over-manicured to such an extent that they almost take on the appearance of a formal Victorian country house water garden. I do not blame this entirely on the resident river keepers, because I believe it is the owners themselves who should communicate to their river keeper to what degree the river should be keepered.

At one time it was strict common practice to cut right down and clear completely the marginal vegetation from along the river banks as soon as the fishing season had ended. No keeper would dare in my early days to leave even the vestige of an upright stem until this chore was completed. I remember so well receiving quite a stiff reprimand from my then employer that the river looked very untidy because by mid-November I had not completed this annual bank clearance! Nowadays the marginal vegetation is hardly touched during the season except for some light trimming and at the end of the fishing season, and the marginal fringe is religiously left to die off naturally through the winter. Whether this policy change significantly improves the habitat for nature to the extent as it is claimed by some is, in my opinion, debatable.

For all the years the river banks on the upper Itchen were cleared completely of vegetation at the end of each fishing season, the fly life during that time was spectacular each season. In the latter years since bankside vegetation has been left untouched, it is noticeable that fly life has not been so prolific! This is surely just coincidence and that the fly reduction should be attributed to other causes, but it does make one think!

Weed cutting in the early days of my river keeping career was a monthly task from April through to November. For a young river keeper it was an ongoing learning process whereby he would soon learn how to efficiently cut weed under water by hand with a sharp scythe. He would learn how to set and sharpen a scythe blade, he would learn which species of weed was better than the next, and he would learn how much weed to cut relative to the ever-changing water flows. A river keeper would learn how to accurately regulate the height of the water in the river by judicious cutting of the right amount of weed. He would learn how to cut weed to manipulate the flows of the river to clear any accumulations of silt, and he learnt how to cut weed to attract trout and provide cover for trout. He learned how to pattern his weed cut in drought years when flows became very low, so water levels were maintained and yet the trout had sufficient space to live in and feed. Lastly, he learned how to cut weed to create good feeding stations for trout within casting distance of the fly fisherman!

He became rather sneaky at times as he also learnt how to cut weed to move vulnerable trout from one feeding station to another safer feeding station out of reach of a fly rod, much to the chagrin of the fly fisherman!

Traditionally the last weed cut of the year was called the autumn cut and tradition decreed that weed was usually cut hard for such reasons as to reduce the incidence of any uncut overwintering tresses of weed being pulled out by the roots by any heavy winter floods and to open up the bed of the river thus enabling the winter flows to cleanse the riverbed.

It was not so many years ago that if any aquatic weed appeared out of the water before or after any weed cut during the fishing season, the river keeper would be severely taken to task for not cutting enough weed. All aquatic weed was expected to be kept well underwater at all times by the river keeper so that fly fishermen had a clear water surface to float his fly and fly line upon without either being caught up by any sprig of emergent weed. How things have changed since those days!

So, have river keeping methods changed over the years and if so what have these changes been, and when and why have they come about?

History teaches us that in most professions apprentices learn their trade from their experienced peers. So it has been in the river keeping profession. Young river keepers sit by the knee of the experienced and learn by word of mouth, practical demonstration, and by observation. Working together with his peer, the young apprentice gradually builds up his knowledge of the river and as his experience grows he becomes more efficient in all he does. The good apprentice will emulate all that his peer does and will even try to do it better. I believe this is where the over-manicuring accusations that are levelled at the chalk streams today stem from. This is because young river keepers learnt what to do and implemented their knowledge, be it good or bad, with boundless youthful enthusiasm aided and abetted by the availability and use of all the wonderful modern mechanised equipment, much of which was not available to his predecessors. Many new river keepers, with their new-found knowledge and enthusiasm, tended to go over the top in all their daily river work of grass cutting, bank clearing and fringe management etc. In most cases the young river keeper wants to make his mark to impress his employer and his fishermen and lastly his compatriot river keepers who happen to visit. To achieve this the river keeper strives hard to be seen to be doing more and a better job than anyone else on the whole river; the result of all this activity inevitably leads to an over-manicured environment around the fishery. Unless controlled from the outset by the owners, this over-manicured state soon becomes established and regarded as standard practice. In many instances this was the case, particularly where river keepers were left to their own devices to keeper the river.

From the early 1800s and right up to the early 1970s, riparian owners and their river keepers had, within reason, virtually complete control on the management of their own waters. The planning, design and implementation of almost all the work involved in the annual and long-term maintenance of a stretch of river was done by the river keeper under the direction of the owner with little controls from outside sources. As long as neighbours had no objections, owners and river keeper did more or less what they liked when they liked on their own waters.

Things started to change with the demise of the regional water authorities and the formation of the National Rivers Authority (NRA) in the early 1980s. The fisheries departments of the new-formed NRA employed scientists and fishery biologists.

The future then looked bright on the chalk streams, but unfortunately the traditionally entrenched river management policies that had evolved and been practiced by the owners and their river keepers for a hundred or so years became a stumbling block for the scientists of the NRA. So much time was spent in discussions and arguments between owners, their river keepers, and the scientists over what should or should not or cannot be done on the rivers that very little was ever achieved.

The NRA was eventually disbanded and its place taken by the present Environment Agency (EA) whose mandate was subtly different to that of the NRA. Fortunately, it was around this time there was a move towards the use of the new science of bioengineering in the protection and maintenance of good habitat and the restoration of degraded habitat in rivers - the pros and cons of which were beginning to be discussed in the UK.

Bioengineering is not just the use of natural materials only, in place of manmade materials like concrete, corrugated iron or steel piles and plastic membranes in and around a river – bioengineering incorporates man's understanding and subsequent use of nature's own materials and its powers to heal.

River keepers of today have to learn to understand like their predecessors did how nature works and by doing so will then be more able to work with nature and not work against nature. 'Let the river teach us' is an old cliché but such an important one for any river keeper to remember. Not until a river keeper understands how and why his whole river works in the way it does can he then begin to help nature to produce or restore the natural flora and fauna of the river over which he has control.

In future the river keeper's role will not be quite so tunnel visioned towards solely producing fish and fishing and maintaining fishing access as it was in the past. The role will of course still include many of these traditional aspects, but these will now be achieved by adopting a softer approach in the implementation by encouraging and using nature to do much of the work. A keeper will also need to be more engaged in the management of the lands adjacent to the river.

Benign neglect may be viewed by some as a positive management tool to use but using it alone is not the way forward. Doing nothing allows nature to run riot. The chalk stream environment, beautiful as it is, is predominantly a manmade environment and if we chose to utilise it in the way we have in the past and want to in the future then that environment must be continually intensively managed to maintain this artificial state.

The traditional river keeping methods of old may change in the future with the growing desire for rivers to look more 'natural' and self-sustaining. Does this mean a river keeper will not be required to do what he used to do? Not a bit of it! Although his role may alter slightly, his work remit to protect, maintain, and restore aquatic habitat will not. A river keeper's work will continue to involve just as much hard work in producing the desired 'keepered wilderness' state that caters for the natural flora and fauna which include fish and fishing access.

CHAPTER 27

OBSERVATIONS ON INVERTEBRATE POPULATIONS OVER 34 WINTERS ON THE UPPER RIVER ITCHEN

My observations over the years have indicated to me that, unfortunately, there has been a decline in the densities of the invertebrate populations on the River Itchen. Although throughout that time the only species to have been extirpated on the upper River Itchen is the Grannom (*Brachycentrus subnubilis*) despite several personal efforts to reintroduce this species by live imports from the River Test.

All the common aquatic insects that we as river keepers and fly fishers cherish are still apparent on the upper Itchen although decreases in species density is becoming more regular by the year, particularly to the more observant who well remember the annually consistent and very prolific fly hatches of fifteen to thirty years ago. The iron blue (*Baetis pumilis*) being the species to take the biggest tumble in density to date.

During my formative years as a river keeper, I was privileged to have been able to sit at the knee of Frank Sawyer on many occasions and listen to his pearls of river keeping wisdom, and besides learning a great deal about practical river keeping of which Frank taught me many things, above all he taught me how to look into a river and to see and understand what was going on. Both the behaviour and life cycles of all the relevant insects has been a fascination to me ever since.

Since retirement, I have from a distance been following with great interest the progress of the Millennium fly Survey that has been co-ordinated by Peter Hayes and Dr Allan Frake.

My contribution, for what it is worth, is taken from my observations over thirty years or more working as a river keeper on the upper Itchen in Hampshire.

Let us start by looking at the optimum spawning times for the wild brown trout of the upper Itchen i.e. last two weeks in December and the first two weeks of January. The best years for spawning intensity, i.e. numbers of completed redds, appeared to occur when heavy autumn and early winter rains had lifted water levels, increased flow speeds, and the river was carrying substantial colour (fines) from the runoff. Personal observations also record that swim up fry survival of trout were far healthier in the spring following these conditions. Furthermore, insect life also improved or was stronger the following season after such a winter. In my opinion, the intensity of prolonged frosts during winter and lower water temperature regimes along with good high river flows carrying colour all contributed to not only good natural production of young of the year trout but also to the resident aquatic insect life.

It became very noticeable whenever there was an open mild winter with low rainfalls, below average winter water flows, higher winter water temperatures and with few, if any, prolonged periods of frost both the young of the year trout survival and insect densities the following spring were much less strong.

In my researches to find some answers to my non-scientific observations, I came across some interesting work by Heede and Rinne (1989) regarding water viscosity.

To quote: "Hydrodynamic variables can help to quantitatively define water flow characteristics. In turn, water flow variables reveal the detailed processes so important to suspended sediment transport, bedload movement, and scour – all of which may positively or negatively affect the quality of the salmonid and insect habitat. Water viscosity has its strongest effect on salmonid and insect habitat through its influence on sediment transport. Viscosity can be envisioned as friction within the water. It is inversely related to temperature and tables exist relating temperature and viscosity. (King 1954) The lower the temperature the greater the viscosity, the greater the sediment transporting capacity of the water. In experiments by Colby (1964) who decreased the water temperature in a flume from 25C down to 4C and because of the resulting increase in water viscosity, sediment discharges characteristic to river sediments increased 254%! Although this may be unrealistic in natural systems it does illustrate the relationship between water temperatures, viscosity and sediment transport. Perhaps therefore it is more than coincidence that salmonids normally spawn during periods of cooler water temperatures. It may also be advantageous for salmonids to spawn during increased sediment transport. Cooler waters would facilitate greater sediment transport than deposition and reduce fine sediment loading of gravels used by spawning trout and insects. Clay fines carried in warmer water may lead to overloading of substrates, as the transporting capacity becomes insufficient to move the fine material through the reach."

My observations on the extreme climatic conditions experienced in Hampshire from the middle/ late 1980s when we struggled through a series of serious low water drought years, through to the early/middle 90s which were accompanied by very high temperatures, low rainfalls and several very mild winters, the combined effects of which could be considered contributory factors for the gradual decline in insect density we are recording today. These extreme conditions could also answer the problems associated in the perceived national decline in *Ranulculas* that was reported by some during the same period, but that is another story.

History teaches that the river gravels of the Itchen, prior to this period, were naturally kept constantly cleaned by good regular high and cool winter flows, and insects would regularly be found living quite happily in clean non-compacted gravel at depths of 12 inches or even more. Today on many waters within the chalk streams and many other lowland rivers, significant areas of constant **clean, silt-free, non-compacted** gravel with depths of one inch or more are becoming harder to find. Increasingly it will be found that these historic areas of gravel used for spawning and insect production which were once naturally kept clean all the year round, have now to be water jetted or hand raked to remove the excessive and more permanent quantities of fine silt that is now being regularly trapped in these substrates. The regular (annual) use of water jetting and hand raking of gravel has yet to be assessed regarding its effects on insect survival. Yet I do have a gut feeling that regular water jetting of spawning gravels may well have a detrimental effect on the survival of the gravel-living insects. This siltation problem can, in chalk streams, be exacerbated by the natural calcification of these fines into an almost concrete-like substrate when and if left undisturbed for longer than one year or more. With this calcification the substrates become virtually impenetrable and so become less attractive to spawning trout and burrowing insects. My observations indicate that wild trout spawning activity in the upper Itchen is far more intensive when the trout are spawning in colder water (2C-5C) that is carrying a deal of colour (fine sediment). In clear warmer water (6C-10C plus) trout spawning activity was found to be far less intensive or exuberant when these conditions occurred during natural spawning times. Furthermore, insect population strengths and young of the year trout survival immediately following these latter winter conditions also appeared to be negatively affected.

My hypothesis is therefore that today's gravel substrates are not being kept naturally so constantly clean as they were 15-30 years or more ago. This fact together with the subtle but important changes in water temperature and rainfall regimes, together with the associated increased fine sediment loading of the gravel substrate, plus the possible long-term effects of chronic non-point source pollutants carried in surface and subsurface catchment runoff, may be contributory factors that could or should be considered in any future efforts to pinpoint and identify the causes of the perceived decline in insect density in the southern chalk streams.

Finally, the effects of the possible subtle climatic changes that may have caused alterations in rainfall and temperature patterns should be examined. For example, although the actual 10 to 20-year average annual rainfall levels may not have altered significantly, the pattern of annual rainfall may show that the same amount of rain still falls annually but in shorter and more intense periods. The effects of these changes could have significant impacts on the sediment loading of runoff which in turn may affect the survival rates of insects.

In my experience this is clearly illustrated in the upper River Itchen catchment, when due to the nature of the geology of the catchment historically, 4" of rain falling evenly over a period of seven days, for example, would cause the river to rise by only an inch or two and yet it would still remain reasonably clear with little heavy sediment loading. However, in my observations, in recent years the general pattern of rainfall and temperatures may have changed with now shorter but more intense periods of rain which even the unique geology of the Itchen catchment can now no longer deal with without discharging significant larger amounts of heavy and fine sediments via the surface runoff. The chalk streams are tending to show more spate-like characteristics these days rather than the traditional calmer spring-fed conditions experienced by river keepers thirty or more years ago.

LITERATURE CITED

Colby, Bruce, R. 1964. Discharge of sands and mean velocity relationships in sand bed streams. USDI Geological Survey. Professional paper 462-A 47p. Washington DC.

King, H.W. 1954. Handbook of hydraulics. 10 Chapters. McGraw-Hill Book Co., Inc, New York.

Burchard H. Heede and John N. Rinne. flowing Water, Stream Form, and Trout Interactions and Implications for Research and Management. Paper presented at Wild Trout IV Symposium. Yellowstone National Park. Wyo., Sept 18-19, 1989.

CHAPTER 28

DOES IT REALLY MATTER WHAT COLOUR LINES WE USE IN DRY FLY FISHING?

This question and a recent letter in the Letters to the Editor column of a fishing magazine requesting fly line manufacturers to consider producing a darker-coloured fly line for dry fly fisherman, prompted me to recall some interesting and quite uncomfortable experiments that I undertook on the waters of the upper Itchen some years ago. This all arose when the subject of fly line colour was being discussed, quite heatedly at times, by some of my more experienced and knowledgeable fisher folk who fished the upper Itchen regularly with me in those days.

Many 'fishing hut' hours were taken up discussing the pros and cons of what these 'experts' thought trout can and do see from their position under the water and particularly what the brown trout's perception of colour might be. In an effort to answer some of these questions for myself, I finally decided to go down to the bed of the river and take a look for myself. To undertake this experiment, which I hoped would put to bed any further discussion on the subject, I raided my own tackle cupboard and my local tackle shop to collect as many different-coloured floating fly lines as I could find. The colours collected ranged from bright white and dull ivory through to the darkest green via peach, blue, red, beige and yellow and various shades thereof. Choosing a warm sunny summer's afternoon when there were no fishermen about, I attached each line to one of the low footbridges that spanned the river and let the lines dangle downstream on the surface of the flowing river. When no one was looking I stripped to my boxer shorts and proceeded to walk into the river and taking a deep breath dipped under the floating lines and whilst holding my breath observed each and every line from the riverbed while looking up to the surface. Even in summer the water temperatures of a chalk stream are such that it shrivels all ones erstwhile valued appendages! However, despite this personal discomfort, the findings of my observations were, for me, quite interesting.

From the very outset it must be understood that we humans do not know for sure the levels of colour perception with which trout are naturally blessed. Clarke & Goddard quote certain academic scientific studies on the trout's perception of colours that were completed by several scientists at the time they wrote their well-known and excellent book *The Trout and the Fly*. However, being rather sceptical by nature, and from my lifetime's experiences with brown trout (both wild and reared stew-bred brown trout), these taught me that it is difficult to agree 100% with Clarke & Goddard on their findings on a trout's perception of colour as they report in their book. Structurally the eye of a trout is somewhat similar to the human eye with a powerful lens, a cornea and an iris. However, the 64,000-dollar question is whether trout see colours as we humans do. I personally very much doubt it, although it has been shown quite conclusively by others that some colours do interest or attract the attention of trout more than other colours, but in my opinion it may be more likely that it is the shades of the colour between dark and bright that fish - trout in particular - appear to respond more readily to. However, in the same token, colours of fly tying materials used to dress flies is a subject that is boundless and will not be discussed here!

To get back to my decidedly chilly observations from the riverbed, firstly I must state the day was bright and sunny. Against the underside of the surface of the water with the bright sky as background, observations from below indicated quite clearly to my human eye that the lighter the colour the line the less obvious it was from the riverbed. However, every line threw the same intensity of shadow onto the bed of the river. So, what can we deduce from this first observation? Not a lot!

If we think about it we will find that almost all freshwater species of fish have white bellies which is a naturally developed form of camouflage to protect these fish from any predators that may attack from below when the fish are lying mid water or feeding off the surface, as in the case of a trout. The markings on the flanks and backs of fish act as camouflage when the fish is laying on the riverbed or is viewed or attacked by predators from the side or above.

Incidentally, as a matter of interest, the intensity of the shade of the natural fixed markings of a trout are determined on the intensity of the darkness of the surrounding habitat within which the trout is living. To illustrate this chameleon-like ability of trout to adapt and match their shade of their skin to their background, I have removed trout from a stew pond that had a black plastic lining to a pond that had pristine clean very light-coloured gravel. It was interesting to observe and watch how quick that trout was to lose its very dark shading and to take on and eventually match the shade intensity of its new bright and light-coloured background. In a matter of minutes, one could determine the changing shade of colour of the flanks and back of that trout as it adapted to its new habitat. Like a leopard, a trout cannot change its spots, so the spots did not change, but it can alter its skin shade very quickly. So, what can this teach us? Again, not a lot! Does it mean that white lines are better to use in bright conditions? Maybe not either!

With further subsurface observations when looking at the lines in different background light intensities and with different colour backgrounds like riverside trees and bankside vegetation and from different angles from below, it will be found that things change somewhat. Viewed from a side angle in bright light, the actual colours of the fly lines were still quite difficult to determine. However, it must be remembered that when viewing from subsurface at any angle sideways that is over 48.5 degrees, then the underside of the surface film becomes a mirror and will only reflect the bed of the river. This is where the laws of reflection and refraction in water come into play and this subject has been discussed and clearly explained in that great and good Clarke & Goddard book already quoted. Not wishing to reiterate all of Clarke & Goddard's findings regarding what they believe the trout can see from below, albeit that a read of their excellent book will enlarge upon the subject for the interested reader. It is important to point out that the field of vision that this angle demands is variable in proportion to depth of the observing eye, i.e. the deeper the eye the wider the field or cone of vision up to the critical 48.5 degrees. However, getting back to my observations, with reduced background light intensity and with a shaded background and keeping the lines within the critical 48.5-degree field or cone of vision, the colours of the fly lines became easier to distinguish from below. It was found that the lighter-shaded colour lines were less obvious and not until it became darker as evening drew in did the darker lines become less obvious as they gradually blended into the darker background light. So, it was not until the real evening arrived did the white lines and the other lighter-shaded lines progressively become more obvious from below. So, again, what can we glean from these rather unscientific observations? Not a lot!

To test the validity of this background and light intensity, try holding at arm's length several bright-coloured pieces of wool up to the sun or to the bright sky and then try with the human eye to accurately distinguish the colour of each separate piece. It is rather difficult to get them all right when there are different shades of the same range of colours. Blues and greens are the most awkward to tell apart. That, however, may be just my perception of colour differentiation. Do we now recommend we all fish with white lines in the daytime and change to a darker-coloured line in the evening? Maybe not!

Having been fortunate to have fished the chalk streams for fifty years or more, I have used during that time green Kingfisher and brown Corona silk lines, and I have used plastic lines of white, peach, yellow, various shades of green and several other colours as and when they appeared on the market. I can honestly say that I have little or no strong reasons that can be measured as to what colour dry fly line is best to use when dry fly fishing on the chalk streams or, in fact, on any other river with a dry fly. Although there may be a good argument to use white lines during bright conditions and I do, in fact, seem to own more white lines than any other colour! However, if asked, I am still convinced that the colour of the line is of little consequence when it comes to fooling wild trout with a dry fly. Although Freud may have something to say about my subconscious preference for white lines for dry fly fishing. To further confound the reader, I must add that one of my working and teaching dry fly rods had a light peach-coloured line on for almost ten years! I seem to use more white lines these days not because they may spook less fish but just because being in the springtime of my senility my eyesight can pick the line out more easily during the evening rise!

I am unable to subscribe to the suggestion that the colour of a fly line puts down wary trout. It's how the angler uses his line, not what colour it is, that counts. Any coloured line will put down trout if you show the line or its shadow to the fish. In my opinion it is the movement of the rod and shade thrown by the rod and line upon the water by the false casting over the water where the target fish is lying that spooks the trout, not the colour of the line. This spooking effect is the same whatever colour line is used. Therefore, it is the honing of the abilities of the angler in his adept stealthy approach and presentation of his dry fly that will determine the level of success. Ideally a good set of dry fly tackle will have a long tapered leader and tippet, and only the very shortest part of which (the fly!) will or should be visible to the trout during the approach and presentation. Lengthen the line over the water, but some way downstream away from the field of vision of the trout, until the right length has been extended and then deliver accurately ('first chuck') the fly at a suitable distance upstream of the target. Trout lying just under the surface have a far smaller cone of vision than a fish that is lying deeper in the water. So usually these fish are more easily approached if the angler can conceal his movements quietly along the river bank and consider the way and where he lengthens his line to make his first delivery cast.

As the use of popular patterns of fly or nymph increases, so the catch rates using these patterns increase in proportion. The same applies to the colour of fly line: the more a certain colour is used the more fish it catches. My experience has taught me that, overall, no one colour line in dry fly fishing catches more fish than any other when used side by side.

Within the realms of still water fishing for trout, fishers of far more experience than me in such matters may have strong views on the most successful colours of fly lines on still water fisheries and it would be of great interest to hear their views, in particular where some subsurface observations have been made in and on still waters. It is felt that the same basic principles apply as described above, although some practical subsurface observations may reveal some other interesting results that may influence the choice of colour of fly lines in still water conditions. To date, the majority of comments I have read regarding the colour of fly lines has been from the angler's viewpoint from above the water and not from what anglers themselves think trout might see from below it.

As mentioned, I do appear to own more white lines than lines of any other colour; in the end all I look for that determines for me the quality of a line is that it has to be supple and not retain any reel memory. It should slide through the rod rings with little effort and has the right profile (taper) suitable to deliver gently and accurately all the fishing casts I wish to make whilst dry fly fishing. What colour has this line to be? Any colour will do!

How do humans who are unfortunately colour blind to the extent of living in a black and white world, come to address the possible colour problems there may be in dry fly fishing? Maybe they cope quite well as shade to me is more important than actual colour. There are various levels of colour blindness but most sufferers, I am told, will usually have a strong perception of shade.

Furthermore, in my experience in dry fly fishing it is the presentation of the artificial to the fish and the size and shape of the artificial that is more important than the actual colour(s) of its tyings.

Colour is a very interesting subject and we all do, I believe, consciously and subconsciously think a great deal about colour in all our various forms of angling and in the design of angling equipment. So, if we want to further discuss the pros and cons of the range of colours and shades of materials now used in fly tying, well then, that is another whole new can of worms!

CHAPTER 29

TO WADE OR NOT TO WADE IN CHALK STREAMS?

Recent correspondence in this magazine over several years has indeed raised some pertinent issues regarding the question of anglers wading or not being allowed to wade in the chalk streams. There are certain considerations which, in my opinion, this correspondence has omitted to mention.

It should be understood that the management practices of our chalk streams do vary quite considerably from one beat to another or from one chalk stream river to the next. That has always been the way, particularly now there are fewer full-time experienced keepers and more part-timers.

The overall intensity of chalk stream management practices has been greatly reduced. For example, the upper Itchen beat at Ovington now must be waded as there is little or no opportunity to fish from the confines of the intensively tree-lined river bank, if you can indeed find a solid river bank under these trees to stand upon! It was not like that 75 years ago!

With sixty years' involvement with the river Itchen management, regimes have changed quite significantly over those years. When I started as a river keeper back in the sixties, when there was a full-time river keeper per mile of the upper Itchen, I was – as all these keepers were – clearly and firmly instructed by the owner how the river was to be managed. In my case the river bank side paths were to be structurally maintained to enable anglers to safely walk along the path without having to resort to wearing waders and entering the water to enable one to fish. The bank grass was to be cut regularly every two weeks by cutting at least three swaths with the Mayfield crosscut grass cutter. The river edge fringe vegetation could grow but was to be kept trimmed to eye height only when kneeling. All other vegetation and trees beyond this path away from the river edge was allowed to grow naturally, although back paths were cut through the dense sedge beds and kept open to allow fishermen access up or downstream on their beat without having to walk the river's edge (therefore avoiding disturbing the water and putting all the trout down for the next few hours!). At times some mature trees were carefully pruned where back casts became impossible. However, a certain number of casting 'bunkers' were purposely left along each beat to challenge a dry fly fisherman's casting expertise from the confines of the dry river bank. With this intensive river bank management any form of wading was strictly 'Verboten'!

With very few full-time river keepers now employed, many bank side paths are now either left uncut or, at the most, only occasionally cut three feet wide and the fringes rarely trimmed at all during the season and many willow trees have been allowed to flourish unchecked. There are few, if any, beats on the upper Itchen that can ever be accused of over-manicuring their river banks. In fact, since moving to Scotland after my retirement, I find some of the salmon beats on the river Tweed are manicured even more intensively than many of the chalk stream beats! In many of the historic keepered beats of the chalk streams no wading has historically been a strict rule to be observed. I agree that the actual damage done to the population survival of aquatic insects by occasional wading would be minimal. However, on the other hand, if there were continually throughout the season numbers of anglers wading to and fro every day across and up and down on one or any of the beats then this continual disturbance of the riverbed and silt and weed beds could well affect the survival rates of the resident invertebrate populations.

A recent picture of an angler wading the 'Penny Lake' carrier on the upper Itchen at Kingsworthy that was published in a fishing magazine earlier this year, clearly illustrates the amount of silt that can be disturbed by just one angler wading. The silt disturbance as illustrated is quite considerable and would soon cover the whole river and seriously affect the fishing below this angler for some considerable distance before it dispersed and the water cleared.

On many an occasion, our fishing has been spoilt by cloudy water caused by anglers a mile or more upstream wading through banks of silty weed, when the river we were fishing should have been gin clear. Instead, the water was cloudy from silt disturbance and thousands of small pieces of weed debris that readily catches the dry fly, all of which had been disturbed and or broken off by thoughtless and inconsiderate anglers wading clumsily on the beats above.

That is just what one does not want when dry fly fishing 'fine and far off' from a river bank for wild trout on the Itchen! The wild trout are hard enough to catch as it is!

CHAPTER 30

SIZE OF FLIES FOR THE UPPER ITCHEN

I remember well in 1959 being despatched by my father to visit Mr Chalkley's tackle shop in The Square in Winchester to purchase a selection of dry flies suitable for fishing the upper Itchen. Father had been invited to fish a beat on the famed upper Itchen and needed some suitable flies for the occasion.

My memory recalls quite clearly that the late Mr Chalkley was a short well-built Victorian gentleman of late age, thinning hair, and wearing a dark three-piece pinstripe suit, black tie, and an ornate gold watch chain suspended across his rotund waist.

For those 'oldies' who remember the famous 'Chalkley's' shop in The Square in Winchester with its large carved wooden fish suspended above the entrance, it was the Mecca for fly fisherman the world over and had been for many years. Along with Hammonds in Jewry Street, Winchester, they were regarded as the tackle shops of the area where all the well-known names associated with the chalk streams had for many years been associated with the evolution of chalk stream dry fly fishing and had frequently patronised the shops to purchase their angling requirements. Halford, Skues, Senior, Marryat et al, all of which were, during their time, regular visitors to Mr Chalkley's wonderful shop.

Having tentatively enquired from Mr Chalkley about dry flies, my attention was directed to an array of trays along one counter that held a selection of dry flies of all various patterns and sizes. Father had not given me any instructions, so I was at a loss which flies to select being at that time young and totally inexperienced in such matters. Mr Chalkley must have noticed the quandary I was labouring under, as he asked me a few questions about where the flies would be used. I told him that the flies were for my father who was a dry fly fisherman who mainly fished the Middle Test and Hampshire Avon. He had been invited to fish a private beat on the upper Itchen somewhere above Martyr Worthy and needed a supply of the appropriate fly patterns. Mr Chalkley immediately directed my attention to a separate tray of dry flies that he said were specifically tied locally for use for the wild brown trout fishing on the upper Itchen. These flies, even to my inexperienced eye, were obviously much smaller than the flies of the other trays on display. All these Itchen flies were tied on size 18 and 20 hooks, whereas the Test flies were all more heavily dressed and tied on much larger size hooks. The numbers used to determine size of hooks in those days were different to the numberings used today, but the difference was just the same. The patterns of these smaller Itchen flies were almost identical to the Test flies except they were much smaller and more lightly dressed.

A decade later, after having been appointed river keeper on the upper Itchen at Martyr Worthy, I was soon to learn from experience that smaller artificial flies than those used on the Test were indeed far more successful on the wild brown trout of the upper Itchen. It should be remembered that there was no grayling in the upper Itchen in those days! Observation over time even suggested to me that some of the natural insects of the upper Itchen were, in fact, also slightly smaller than the same natural insects of the Test. One particular species, the iron blue dun, caught my attention. This species, which appeared in great numbers each spring on the upper Itchen, was indeed smaller than the natural iron blue dun that appeared at the same time on the Test. These observations regarding the iron blue were corroborated by the legendary Dermot Wilson and Gus Headlam, both of whom were recognised doyens of the dry fly and were for many years regular tenants on the water where I was privileged to be river keeper.

It is noted in John Goddard's recent article, where he mentions that both he and Peter Lapsley, who fish the upper Itchen, together tie their flies and nymphs on 12 or 14 hooks when fishing for grayling. If they use these hook sizes for grayling on the Itchen it is logical to suspect that they may also be using the same size dry fly and nymph hooks for trout on the same waters. I agree with John Goddard's comments that smaller size flies and nymphs should be used. By using smaller dry flies and nymphs tied on 18s and 20s, or even 22s, it could improve sport on the upper Itchen.

CHAPTER 31

WILD BROWN TROUT, NATIVE BROWN TROUT AND STOCKED BROWN TROUT ARE ALL SALMO TRUTTA SO WHAT, IF ANY, ARE THE DIFFERENCES?

I remember so vividly at one of the early meetings of the Wild Trout Society (WTS) which was soon to become the Wild Trout Trust (WTT), participating in a very lively discussion between my fellow co-founders of the WTS. The discussion was to answer the 64,000-dollar question "What is a wild brown trout?" for no better reason than we had to determine an answer to the question as we had that day just formed the Wild Trout Society!

After many fag breaks, cups of coffee, and serious head scratching, we finally came up with the following description which has since been universally accepted as the Wild Trout Trust's definition of a wild brown trout.

WILD BROWN TROUT

"A wild brown trout is a trout that completes its life cycle without direct help from humans after hatching in a largely natural environment from eggs deposited there by its mother. The progeny of these eggs rear to maturity, spawn and have offspring to produce the next generation of wild trout."

It should be understood, that although the parents of these trout may have come from planted stock fish, their offspring as described are deemed to be wild trout.

It is suggested that many of us anglers inadvertently confuse 'wild trout' with 'native trout'. So, are there any differences? The decision is yours!

A NATIVE BROWN TROUT

A wild brown trout can be described as above, whereas a native brown trout is significantly different and is recognised as such – as being a member of a population of trout that completes its breeding cycle uninterrupted by man or by any untoward stocking introductions and has done so continually in the same location since the end of the last ice age when brown trout first colonised UK waters from the European continent, to which these islands were then attached. Wild trout are therefore not necessarily native trout. Surprisingly, there are many distinct populations of native brown trout that have been identified by researchers in the UK that fall into this 'native' category and I am led to understand more discrete populations could yet be identified.

As fly fishers we should remember that all the brown trout in our waters – whether stocked, wild or native – belong to the widely distributed yet close-knit family *Salmo trutta*. With the development of modern DNA science and technology and the progress made in the science of genetic research in fish, fishery managers have been able to identify and learn much more about the many and varied strains of brown trout that exist in many of our waters within the UK.

The study and understanding of brown trout genetics is an intricate branch of fisheries science - much of which, I must confess, is way above my head. There is one thing I have learnt and that is the genetic profile of a brown trout population can be simply described as the historic ecological memory of that population. Scientists are now able to extract a trout's DNA and from that determine and understand quite accurately the way the population itself has, over time, fitted into and adapted to its particular environment better and better in each generation. We also understand that these heritable traits are recorded in the DNA of the fish and so handed down from generation to generation.

Numerous individual known strains of brown trout are now dispersed over the world and these can be known by such names as Loch Leven, Test, Itchen, Loch Awe, German and so on. Man, in his wisdom, has transported representatives of these strains of brown trout around the world and introduced them into waters on every continent of this Earth. No matter which strain was used in these introductions, in order to survive successfully the survivors had to adapt to the local prevailing ecological conditions of the receiving waters. From these early survivors, subsequently over several generations grew a new self-sustaining brown trout population. Many of these populations have been established around the world which can now be recognised as wild brown trout, but native brown trout they are certainly not!

These introduced strains of trout may lose their historic genetic 'pedigree', but they normally retain all the beautiful and much cherished recognisable external physical features of a typical brown trout.

A STOCKED BROWN TROUT

The least wild and most intensively managed trout populations are of catchable trout or, as more commonly called, 'put and take' trout. These trout are of domesticated parents, raised in the sterile confines of a hatchery, fed on special food and when of required size are then ferried to a river, lake or reservoir and released.

HOW DO WE RECOGNISE A WILD BROWN TROUT WHEN WE CATCH ONE?

Here I stick my head above the parapet with the risk of having it shot off!

If a caught trout is to be returned unharmed then only a quick examination of its external features can be undertaken whilst in the net prior to release. In the case of a stocked trout, in most cases a quick glance at the quality of its fins may give a good indication whether the fish is wild or stocked. This is not at all scientifically accurate as authoritative biological checks cannot be done on the river bank! However, to the experienced eye of any fly fisher who has worked with or fished for wild fish, stocked fish or native fish for any length of time will soon become reasonably adept at determining wildness by observation of the body shape and the condition of the fins of a fish. From this cursory visual examination, the experienced fisher can soon learn to determine quite accurately whether the fish is stocked or wild. Wild fish and native fish in good health would normally exhibit the standard body shape and perfect quality fin conditions typical of the species. Unless stocked trout are introduced at the swim up fry stage of their life, or at latest at month fed stage, any introductions thereafter at any older life stage will generally mean these fish usually display some fin wear or fin malformation, although natural fin regeneration can at times make this difficult to identify. To test this hypothesis, take one known genuine fresh wild trout and lay it beside a fresh known stocked trout of similar size. Before the fish have dried out, study very carefully and compare, identify and note any discernible differences in the body shape, condition and completeness and thickness of each fin and the fineness of the leading edges of all the fins. Any differences in most cases, even to an inexperienced eye, soon become obvious.

Of the many rivers in the UK, some still have a resident population of native or self-sustaining wild brown trout albeit at times now mere remnants of historical larger stocks. This is despite many years of degrading habitat and/or considerable heavy stocking of stock fish over these populations. In the heavily stocked areas of the Test and/or Middle Itchen, for example, there are some resilient resident brown trout who appear to survive quite happily and relatively unpolluted by any excessive breeding with stock trout. Be these wild trout or remnants of native trout is yet to be substantiated! The possible controlling factor of the small size of these populations usually can be pinpointed in the poor or limited available spawning facilities. Is nature trying to tell us something?

There is a very interesting corollary to this observation on the chalk streams that has come to light in Loch Awe in Scotland, where three very distinct strains of native brown trout have been identified. Genetic studies of these trout indicate that these individual populations of native brown trout have lived side by side in the same loch for thousands of years, yet they have retained their separate and very distinct individual genetic profile. They apparently spawn in different areas and do not excessively interbreed and yet live happily together in the same loch. There is still much we do not know about the trout we fish for, particularly *Salmo trutta*.

As for rainbows in the UK, that is a very different story as there is predominantly now a mish-mash of strains of rainbow made up from landlocked Shasta and Kamloops strains and anadromous steelheads, all of which have been imported into the UK over time from the west coast of America. Hatchery managers in the UK have mixed these together to produce the ubiquitous 'rainbow', now generally designated *Onchoronchus mykiss*. Rarely, if ever, do these rainbow introductions into UK waters breed successfully once released into the wild. I am also quite convinced these twenty first century rainbows do not now possess the historical physical dynamism or stunning good looks once exhibited by their early immigrant forefathers. In the USA there still remain, thankfully, many healthy self-sustaining populations of the various strains of 'rainbow' etc. that have not been diluted by improper introductions, and I am reliably informed that there are also many rivers in British Columbia up to Alaska and down the West Coast of the USA, not to mention Northern Russia and the Kamchatka Peninsula, which still have vast unpolluted and virtually unexploited runs of native steelheads, so I cannot support the uninformed notion held by some angling writers in the UK that all rainbow stocks in the USA have been corrupted!

CHAPTER 32

WHAT MAKES A GOOD GAME ANGLING INSTRUCTOR?

Having been a qualified game angling instructor for more years than I wish to remember, thirty-six so I was informed recently, there are a few things that need to be clarified for any person who has a desire to become a game angling instructor. Other than the Association of Advanced Professional Game Angling Instructors (AAPGAI), there are other organisations within the UK who also offer qualifications as coaches or instructors in game fishing, unfortunately all of which have differing levels of technical requirement in their syllabi and all have assessing standards that are inconsistent. The angling public, in my opinion, are being misled by these organisations into thinking that the instructors the organisations qualify are highly trained instructors when, in fact, they are not. A suitable analogy that springs to mind illustrating the difference there is between most of the qualifications these organisations offer and those offered by AAPGAI is like comparing an O-level to a BSc. Unfortunately, any member of the public who may seek to hire a qualified instructor to teach them to fly fish is unaware of the differences there are between these organisations and their qualifications.

There is a popular misconception held by some, who think that being AAPGAI qualified means that AAPGAI instructors are expert casters only. Nothing can be further from the truth. AAPGAI is not merely a casting organisation. Qualified AAPGAI instructors teach all aspects of game angling, including fly tying.

Of course, a very high standard of casting is required to be demonstrated by every candidate at every stage of the AAPGAI qualification process. Being able to cast well alone is still not enough, as the successful candidate has to demonstrate, explain and teach the use of each cast and where and when and how it should be used. The candidate must be able to clearly and efficiently instruct and explain the mechanics of any particular cast to a student. Casting brilliance alone is not enough without the required good communication and teaching skills, and all-round knowledge of all aspects of game angling is required to become an AAPGAI game angling instructor. Nothing undermines a beginner's confidence more than being overwhelmed by a show off casting instructor! Casting is important of course, but it is only one of the many other equally vital abilities required of an AAPGAI qualified game angling instructor.

Since its formation, AAPGAI has worked to improve the technical content of its syllabi at every level of qualification. This is an ongoing process that keeps up to date with all the new tackle and new casting methods that appear each year. AAPGAI qualifications are now recognised worldwide as the highest standard available. Any qualification is only as good as the assessors who assess the candidates. With that in mind, AAPGAI have established a comprehensive three-year assessor training process which includes an external assessment by an official independent assessor scheme (City & Guilds L20) that ensures all AAPGAI assessments, at whatever level, are undertaken by fully trained assessors in a professional manner that ensures every assessment of a candidate is of a consistent high standard.

To qualify for the AAPGAI core qualification, the 'Advanced' candidate needs to have extended his/her provisional casting abilities to cover all the added requirements in the 'Advanced' syllabus. The candidate has also to demonstrate his/her depth and breadth of knowledge and experience of every aspect of game angling in a written exam paper. The candidate will have an intensive oral interview which will discuss a range of subjects from conservation, entomology, angling law, fish biology etc. The candidate has also to present a prepared practical thirty-minute demonstration to an audience on a game angling subject of choice. The written paper, presentation and interview all carry percentage marks towards attaining a pass or a fail. An AAPGAI instructor who has attained the 'Advanced' level of qualification, besides being passed as a good caster and efficient casting instructor, will have demonstrated to the assessors to have a wide knowledge of and be conversant with every aspect of game angling. This will enable him/her in the future to confidently and efficiently discuss and instruct or give advice on any of the recognised forms of game angling.

All AAPGAI members are required to maintain and improve their skills after attaining the Advanced Certificate, by attending regular CPD events to ensure that they remain 'on top of the game'.

As there is more to fly fishing than catching fish, so there is more to game angling instruction than casting! Being recognised as a great caster or a show platform casting demonstrator does not always mean the caster is a good efficient instructor!

For anyone who is interested in becoming a qualified game angling instructor, I suggest they Google up AAPGAI on the internet and trawl through their comprehensive and informative website.

CHAPTER 33

THE 'KISS' PRINCIPAL IN THE MANAGEMENT OF HABITAT FOR WILD TROUT

Like most things in life, the simpler the strategy usually the more efficient it is. So, the 'KISS' principal (Keep It Simple, Stupid!) can be applied to the management of the habitat for wild trout. Basic common sense is all that is needed to improve wild trout survival once it is understood what needs to be done. For the sake of this brief discussion we will assume that the water quality is such that trout can flourish. Therefore, the first thing that is required is a good and thorough understanding of the entire life cycle of the wild brown trout from egg through to mature adulthood. The life stages are: egg, alevin, swim up fry, parr, fingerling and mature adult. Most trout anglers will already know this through close observation whilst fishing for trout or they will have read about it. With this knowledge on board, it is a simple exercise of observation aided by the use of a fishing rod at times to pinpoint the areas within the water where each of the free swimming life stages of the trout are to be regularly found. With this closer inspection it will soon be discovered that each life stage favours different areas within the whole watery habitat that is available, other than the eggs which are in a fixed position once laid and buried under the gravel by the adult trout and the alevin which emerges from the egg and lives in and under the gravel until its yoke sac has been absorbed before it swims up through the gravel to emerge as a swim up fry. It should be noted where and what all these different habitats provide and which element of it attracts the trout to live within it.

A healthy self-sustaining wild or native trout population needs good and constant water quality, cover, food and spawning facilities for it to thrive in a robust state. Once each of the life stages of the trout have been identified, it should be understood that at some period within each life stage there will be a factor or factors, usually due to a lack of something, which controls the survival rates of that life stage. By good observation the preferred living quarters of each life stage will be identified and soon it should become evident where and what the **limiting factor(s)** controlling survival is or are, so the appropriate action can be taken.

Even in the most productive wild trout waters it will be found that there is somewhere a limiting factor that regulates the survival rates of the resident fish population at each life stage. The art and success of any fishery manager or river keeper is measured in his ability to identify these limiting factors and in mitigating them at each life stage and in such a way that increases survival of that life stage to move on to the next.

So, by looking at **each** life stage requirement for good survival, habitat improvements can be planned that will not only provide more of the right habitat but will also encourage and provide more of the right food. Trout need to feel safe from predators with good hiding places to use, with feeding areas close to hand, a plentiful food supply readily available and good clean well-aerated gravel readily accessible where they can spawn. The life cycle of the wild trout can be compared with an endless circular chain where each link represents a life stage of the wild trout. Identify the weakest link but don't say goodbye to it! Instead, strengthen it and then identify the next weakest link and strengthen that one and so on ad infinitum. Care for, maintain, protect, enhance and restore good habitat where necessary and the wild trout will respond and do the rest.

There are also predators at each life stage to consider. The survivors from each life stage will continually be subjected to predation from many quarters. From stonefly and mayfly nymphs, eels, perch, pike, chub and avian predators of many species, to even adult brown trout themselves who will all feast on the young of trout at some stage. A fit adult hen trout will lay approximately 1000 eggs for every pound of her body weight and even in ideal conditions only around half of 1% of the content of those eggs will survive through to celebrate their first birthday. Survival rates do of course vary year to year with some years better than others, but that is the way nature works.

CHAPTER 34

A TYPICAL 'WHITE STRING DAY' ON THE ITCHEN!

A few years back at Martyr Worthy where I was at the time the river keeper, we had as one of our tenants a gentleman who I shall call Peter, who was not only a very good dry fly fisherman but also was very knowledgeable about wine and was an expert in consuming quality wine!

Peter enjoyed entertaining fishing friends on the river and often had the company of a good fishing friend whenever he came to fish. He would phone me the day before to say he is coming the next day and would be bringing a friend and could I meet them on the car park at 10am. Spot on 10am a car would arrive, and I would unload the lunch hamper and the wine hamper and stagger down to the fishing hut whilst they carried all their fishing gear. Having stowed the food hamper into the shade of the hut, I would open the wine hamper and find several bottles of quality white Burgundy - usually one of the Montrachet wines. Along with wine there would also be nine wine glasses and a ball of white string and a cork screw (although, as with any good river keeper, I was never without my Swiss Army knife in my pocket which had a cork screw!). My job then was to take three bottles of wine and the nine glasses up to the first footbridge just above the hut from where Peter and his guest would start fishing. I would leave three wine glasses upside down on the bridge decking and tie a length of white string to a bottle of wine and gently lower it into the river and tie it off to the hand rail of the bridge. I would then move up to the next footbridge some 200 yards further upstream and do the same and again at the top bridge some 300 yards further upstream.

On returning to the hut, rods would have been put up and reels and lines and leaders checked before deciding what fly should be used. With all these usual preambles completed, off they would go to fish - one on the left-hand bank and the other on the right-hand bank. I usually accompanied the guest and acted as ghillie, particularly if he was not conversant with this part of the river. If I was not required I would sit and watch them fish. That is until either of the fishermen reached the first bridge before the other, where the strict routine was to stop fishing and wait until the other fisherman had fished his way up to the bridge. My job then was to retrieve the bottle of wine from the river by handlining the bottle up by the white string; the wine by this time had been suitably chilled to perfect drinking temperature. With a swift turn and pull of the cork screw, three glasses were filled, one each for the two fishermen and the other for the keeper, and the wine was sampled and drunk whilst sitting on a bench beside the footbridge. Corks were never replaced in wine bottles whenever Peter was fishing! It was now 11am and still there were two more bridges to go before a very long lunch which would be taken back at the hut, accompanied by a classic red wine that had been left to chambre in the shade of the hut. Being high summertime there would be very little fishing done in the afternoons! Time would be spent talking, telling stories or just gossiping. Although I do recall one afternoon when the fish were going crazy, the same performance was repeated in the afternoon... that day Peter and his guest did not return for the evening rise... I wonder why!

This routine became so regular that Peter would ring me the day before and just say, "White String Day, tomorrow, 10am".

My only comment that I made that Peter still remembers is when we were leaving the river one day I said to his departing guest, "The River Itchen is the perfect river for chilling white Burgundy to the right temperature... it also can used for fishing!"

It can be hard life being a river keeper... but someone must do it.

CHAPTER 35

EQUALITY FOR GRAYLING IN CHALK STREAMS, NO THANKS!

It should be made clear that grayling, albeit considered a wonderful game fish and deservedly so in their own right in their own natural environment, are however an alien species in the chalk streams. Grayling were introduced into the chalk streams by man not by nature.

Rarely, if ever, has any introduced species by man into any environment not had some negative impact on the receiving waters and its resident fish species. The interaction between an introduced alien species and the resident species of fish rarely can be shown to be a positive one.

Knowing many experienced chalk stream fly fishers as I do, I am confident most of those anglers have the greatest respect and regard for grayling in waters where they are indigenous and have, since the last ice age, lived and thrived side by side with wild trout.

It is therefore of no great surprise that fishery managers and many anglers on the chalk streams regard grayling as intruders or even vermin. Particularly where anglers and fishery managers can clearly remember how superb the wild trout fishing was before the grayling were introduced.

If nature had intended grayling to be in the chalk streams, then they would have arrived there naturally by their own means as the brown trout did as soon as the last ice age receded and not as they have in recent years via a stocking truck.

CHAPTER 36

UNUSUAL EXPERIENCE WITH A KINGFISHER

The kingfisher is a magnificent bird and many anglers who fish in freshwater have seen them at some time or other when they have been fishing. That brilliant flash of blue and chestnut as it arrows its way along a river and its unmistakable "peep" as it flies past, once seen and heard is unforgettable. Many anglers, particularly coarse fishermen who lay their rods on rod holders while ledgering, often tell of the time a kingfisher had perched on one of their fishing rods while suspended over the water. It is different with fly fishers as their rods are moving most of the time.

My most unforgettable encounter with a kingfisher was not with a fishing rod.

I used to rear trout from eggs taken from some wild trout netted out of the river and would hatch these eggs and rear fish up to takeable size to sell to other parts of the Rivers Itchen and Test.

There was a series of disused watercress beds at the bottom of my garden beside the river, where I could rear young trout on good pure spring water that flowed unceasingly out of the chalk. I had placed a ten-foot fry trough into the gravel where I was able to channel this spring water through the trough. I would transfer the alevins from my hatchery into this trough just as the alevins were turning over into swim up fry. That is when the alevin had almost used up its yoke sac. It is a critical time if good survival is to be expected, as getting these fries to start to feed on artificial food can be rather tricky at times. Initially I would feed these fry every two hours during daylight. The trough was covered with a board to restrict the light over which there was a fine mesh netting to keep out predators. I would fold back the netting and slide the board back about 18 inches which allowed me to gently sprinkle some proprietary fry food granules into the top end of the trough. Just a pinch at a time to start with until the fry became aware that these granules were food. This process would take about twenty minutes.

One morning as I was stood almost motionless astride the trough looking down at the fry at my feet, slowly sprinkling a pinch of food into the trough, something caught my eye. A kingfisher had perched on a willow herb stalk that was hanging over the bank of the old cress bed. It was just ten feet away from me. I froze and tried not to blink, let alone move a muscle. The bird bobbed a couple of times on its swinging perch as I watched. I was able to see every feather of its brilliant plumage and its bright alert eyes. I expected the bird to fly off, but no, it did not fly off and what happened next is something I shall never ever forget: it flew from its perch and landed on my left shoulder, only inches from my cheek; I even felt the air move as it alighted. It only stayed for a second or two before it dived down between my feet into the open fry trough and took several fry in its beak and flew back to its perch on the willow herb stalk where it quickly tapped the fry against its perch and promptly swallowed them. Still motionless, I watched the bird as it continued to bob up and down on its perch. *It would not do that again,* I thought to myself... and no, it did not, it then flew off down the river.

Many times since, I have thought about that incredible experience and wished someone could have witnessed the event. Furthermore, I have often wondered how that kingfisher knew that there were trout fry in that trough as the trough had only been in place for a couple of days. I will never know. Nature is a wonderful thing!

CHAPTER 37

BEWARE: CIGARETTES ARE BAD FOR YOUR FLY LINES!

Although I should not, I do smoke, and I do smoke whilst dry fly fishing. One becomes adept in holding a fly rod and loose line and extracting a cigarette and lighting it all at the same time.

I happened to be watching one of my fisherman fishing one morning; the trout were rising quite steadily, and he had marked a good fish. I watched as he crept up on his hands and knees behind the cover of the fringe of bank side vegetation that I leave uncut just for such situations. He was now in range, so he waited patiently for the trout to rise again. With a figure of eight bunch of line in his left hand and his rod in his right hand with a finger trapping the line to the rod, the leader and fly plus a couple of feet of fly line out of his rod tip waving free in the air, he waited. Time for a fag... so as only an expert fly fishing smoker can do, with his hands full he extracted a cigarette and lit it whilst crouched down on one knee. As he waited for the action to start, he slowly smoked his cigarette with his left hand that held the bunched line.

A few minutes later the trout rose and as it did he lifted his rod, made a false cast or two to extend his line, then shot the loose line he was holding towards the fish, after he had parked his cigarette into his mouth whilst he cast. To his utter astonishment, the line with leader and fly flew out over the water and did not stop until it collapsed in a heap halfway across the river, where the current picked it up and took it off down the river never to be seen again! It transpired on close examination that his line had been severed by his cigarette somewhere between his right hand that was trapping his line to his rod handle and before the figure of eight bunch of line he held in his left hand. Fortunately, he had a spare reel and floating line in his bag, so after some considerable laughter he continued to fish but decided it would be a good idea not to smoke whilst fishing, as Cortland 444 floating lines are quite expensive!

CHAPTER 38

SOME PHILOSOPHICAL REFLECTIONS ON THE FUTURE MANAGEMENT OF THE WILD TROUT OF THE UK

A great deal has been discussed recently in the angling media about the benefits that scientists may or may not bring to the game fish resources of the British Isles. The hypothesis presented here is that the time is fast approaching when the trout fishing world will witness the mating of the philosopher and the scientist, and the indications are that the seeds of this coition have already been sown in many places.

For a dedicated angler who has relished the sport of fly fishing for wild trout for 50 years or more, it would certainly be exciting to be around after this union has taken place. The progeny of this marriage could well be wild trout fishing, the like of which may rarely have been seen before, let alone sampled. The scientist may be the breadwinner of this union, but the philosopher will wear the trousers! Once the goals have been set by the philosopher, the scientist will take over in order to achieve the desired end which is quality wild trout and quality wild trout fishing.

The demand for the finest possible fly fishing stems from the dedicated hobbyists, the individuals who really care for wild trout fishing. They are the ones who lavish time and money on this recreation. As travellers of the wide world or as more local regular customers, they are the free spenders and therefore of considerable value to others. When they hear of some quality trout fishing they yearn to sample it, and when they find what they like they usually return to it time and time again. Thus, it is not only their desires that are so vitally important to the many non-fishermen who are involved in the economic interests related directly or indirectly to fishing but also to those who dedicate their lives to the protection, maintenance and restoration of wild trout and wild trout habitat.

To the dedicated angling hobbyist, fly fishing for wild trout never was, or ever will be, a simple affair. The true greatness of this most enjoyable of human occupations is due to many features: the fascination of the problems presented, the beauty of the environment of wild trout, the accumulation of knowledge, the honing of the powers of observation and analysis, the gaining of implemental skills - all combine to meet the challenge of imitation, presentation and water craft; all of which can, at times, be so bloody complicated!

Each trout stream, burn or loch presents its own individual problems to be solved, and all its varied moods and mannerisms need to be understood by the angler. A rising trout of some proportions is the ultimate to which the dedicated fly fisherman's eye is tuned, his ear cocked and his fly cast. Given this situation the discerning angler is kept in total absorbed delight as time gently passes by but, unfortunately, on many of our historic classic trout waters these days it is now a hoped for rather than an expected event.

In the evolution of modern man the hunter gatherer instincts are still latent in humans, because each generation in turn produces offspring cast in the mould of its progenitors and there exists therein a strong desire at times to follow in their footsteps. Each generation in turn hears the call that has reverberated through the aeons of time. Anglers answer this deeply ingrained and powerful pull when the blood is stirred as the heart starts to race on the discovery of a large wild brown trout rising to a natural surface-borne fly just within casting distance.

Let us briefly take a closer look at today's discriminating descendent of early man who now waves a featherweight carbon fibre wand as he stalks his way slowly up the banks of a favourite trout burn or drifts across his chosen Highland loch or Midland reservoir. We soon find that herewith there is a very strange paradox. In fact, it must be the strangest for any known sport on Earth and something that appears so positively confounding to the non-angler.

This lone fly fisherman sets forth to catch wild trout, but he does not want to catch them too easily. He likes to catch large ones, but he does not want them to be the same size. He does not like the experience of fish getting away, but he does not want to be too successful in landing every fish he rises or hooks. Just because he is in pursuit of trout does not mean he must kill all he catches, as this is reducing every fish to a state of possession, which inevitably leads to the modern affliction of 'limititis'! There must be a certain degree of failure and a considerable amount of uncertainty. The degree of personal satisfaction is realised in the wonderful challenge presented by the natural problems and the immense satisfaction gained in the solving of these problems – this, in essence, is what fly fishing for wild trout is all about.

Increasingly it will be found that almost all quality trout fishing is under great people-pressure today and this comes in many and varied forms. One is reserved for holiday times that involves a dedicated destination trip to some primitive place. The fish may not be sophisticated, but there will be peace and solitude and natural beauty in abundance. Such trout fishing is like gold dust – it is where we find it. But as enjoyable as these trips may be, they will not suffice for the regular angler. He must be able to fish more regularly than just at holiday time. So, this other type of fishing must be within easy reach. It must be available for weekend fishermen and the one-day-a-week fisher, or just for evening times. Indeed, it is a fortunate angler who today can regularly ponder long on the banks of a favourite trout stream or tread the shores of his local loch and leisurely fish through the ebbing pulse of a dying summer's day.

With all this added pressure, what of the wild trout? They too have their ways of learning and here the laws of survival of the fittest prevails, as it does naturally with the wild red grouse, red fox, red deer and badger. Harassment and danger is what fishing pressure is all about. It trains wild trout to be shy, observant, alert and resourceful; it encourages them to develop hyper caution. The common word for this is 'leader shy' and that phrase was not coined without reason! For anglers to understand, we must allow wild trout to become sophisticated by giving them a second chance to benefit from their youthful exuberance and misjudgement. So now add to this the economic truism that a wild trout is too valuable to use only once!

It is at this stage the philosopher swings into action as the scientist searches out the facts, and as and when their two travel paths cross there will be a union resulting in a new dimension in the protection, management and production of quality fly fishing for wild trout.

It is understood today that chief among the frustrations and vexations of many a distraught fly fisher is the matter of where to go for some quality fly fishing for wild trout. This perceived union of philosopher and scientist will address this problem by stimulating special trout management.

The whole purpose here is to explore the possibilities that will result in the positive protection and management of our wild trout and wild trout fishing in Scotland, in spite of diminishing natural resources, modern development, and poor land use management and, in places, non-existent or inept fishery management regimes.

Experience teaches that the most important fish to the wild trout fly fisherman are the surface feeders, as they become prime targets as they advertise themselves of the fact they are on the feed.

Among the major problems that have to be addressed is what happens when the insect life disappears, or when the most valuable wild fish both of catchable size and their brood stock are eventually removed by overexploitation? What happens when fish populations are lost by unprotected and degrading habitat and are replaced by flaccid pellet-fed stock fish who have little or no experience of feeding off the surface, even if they had the chance?

The philosopher will continue to philosophise and as like breeds like so after the habitat has been restored let's let the scientist apply Mendel's law to produce the right strain of free rising trout. Once the scientist understands our problems and recognises his assignment his tasks are not all that difficult, and he likes them because they are of interest to him for the future. He is so different from the commercial hatchery man! However, the philosopher has to realise that there is more than the quality of our fishing and trout that has to be subject to management.

The greatest predator of all is man himself and he does at times present a problem. By intellect though he is still the conservationist, therefore the required plan must be clearly explained to him so there will be support and understanding in all we seek to achieve.

The education could start by asking that there should be no killing of the undersized wild free risers and they should be returned to grow on. The take home rewards to consist of the odd prize fish that would be past its sell by date if returned to overwinter once more.

The angling philosopher will at this stage quote the patron of all aquatic conservationists, Aldo Leopold, who wrote, "There must be management which will positively produce rather than negatively protect. Wildlife is a crop which Nature will grow abundantly provided we furnish the right seeds and the suitable environment."

These axioms are inseparable when considering wild trout and the management of the environment for them.

Anyone who has spent the best part of his working life on and around a wild trout river understands that nature is indeed a hard taskmaster, but nature is also a very willing servant but the opportunities she offers must be recognised before they can be grasped.

Experienced practical 'hands on' wild trout fishery management frontiers must spill over into biology and other related sciences if there is to be any positive development in wild trout management. Once achieved, many problems can be solved and the main one, 'better fishing', is simplicity itself when compared to man's ability to split the atom and cruise around in space and land on the moon.

Our precious wild trout lochs, lochans, rivers, streams and burns do need special attention because new ones are just not being made any more. The character and value and quality of many of our historic and revered wild trout lochs, lochans, rivers and burns are in jeopardy. In the name of progress some are in greater danger than others and could suffer ruination by overexploitation, misguided and ill-informed management, and poor catchment land use practices. There must be a recognition of their monetary value for quality recreational pursuits as well as for preservation and conservation.

In many of the more remote areas of this country there is a strong feeling that the wild brown trout populations are still in excellent condition, and there is little doubt that this is the case in some catchments. In consequence, unfortunately, few, if any, future management plans are deemed to be required and it is concluded that therefore nothing should be done. However, similar complacent 'do nothing' opinions were held by many during the latter half of the twentieth century on the lowland chalk rivers of England, and history painfully teaches us that many of those streams have since continued to pay dearly from such high-powered inertia.

It might be constructive to encourage the fishery managers and scientists in these remote areas to take off their rose-tinted glasses and look more towards planning for the protection of what they still have left by building and being part of a broader long-term science-based wild trout strategy for the whole of Scotland – a strategy, once formulated, to be embedded into each individual integrated catchment management plan. Until such times arrive, in the interim it is essential that energies be committed to the protection of what there is still left rather than repairing damage or doing nothing at all. History also teaches us that each pennyworth of protection is worth £100 of restoration.

Considered serious thought therefore has to be given to the discriminating wild trout angler who is an angling philosopher by nature, because it is only their hope and their care and concern for our natural wild trout resources that will determine the future health and strength of the wild trout populations of this country. From here on, in our wild trout waters, it has to be '**re-creation for recreation**'. There should be no fear that the fishing tackle of our children and their children's children will be a personal computer, a Playstation and a virtual reality package on fly fishing for wild trout!

What is needed in the wild trout world of today is a meeting of the minds of the philosopher and the scientist – that's all.

CHAPTER 39

INTERESTING PEOPLE ONE MEETS BESIDE THE RIVER

There have been many fascinating experiences over the years meeting and fishing with some very interesting and well-known people. Many of which were and still are well-known household names and come from the many walks of the public, political, industrial, sporting, military and artistic world. There can be few occupations like a river keeper that offers so many opportunities of meeting and studying such a wide variety of people. So often it will be found that the public perception of the persona of many of these prominent people so markedly changes after meeting and fishing with them away from the public eye. Fly fishing with these people gives one an excellent insight into the real character of such people, many of whom in their everyday environment portray a totally different persona.

Having been an average yet keen club cricketer, it was a great privilege to have discussed at great length the ups and downs of the England sides Test match performance against Australia with a current county cricket captain who was a regular guest of one of the tenants. There are also vivid memories of telling the assembled members at the bar of Winchester rugby club that I had recently spent a whole day fishing with one of the best (if not *the* best) Welsh international fly half in history!

One charming visitor who comes to mind was at the time the then current 'Black Rod' in the Houses of Parliament. That was a wonderful memorable day spent in his company and I well remember being captivated by some of the accounts of his experiences whilst carrying out the duties of his historic position within the palace of Westminster. The fascinating history associated with his position and his duties held me spellbound for most of the day spent in his company and opened my eyes to much of the priceless heritage and traditions upon which this country of ours has evolved.

Away from the river bank at a game fair some years ago, I vividly remember being introduced to a prominent member of the royal household who happened to be a very keen fly fisher and fly tier. Having sported a luxuriant growth of mutton chop whiskers for forty years or more I was immediately quizzed on the potential of my whiskers for tying up some hair wing salmon flies for use on Royal Deeside!

Less memorable were some guests during the financial boom and bust years of the 1980s in the city markets where fortunes were made and lost by wheelers and dealers on the stock market long before the dot com and hedge fund era. Fishing with some of these wheelers and dealers did become quite hard work at times, especially when fortunes had been recently lost on some precarious investment. 'Black Thursday', sometime in 1988 I think it was, still stands out in my mind when things in the city went topsy-turvy. After which several once-familiar faces were never seen again on the river!

It is quite surprising to some that several well-known rock stars fly fish. One in particularly became a regular rod on the Martyr Worthy water for many years and subsequently became a good friend. Sat in one of the fishing huts over a tin of beer listening to his reminiscence of his early years in the 60s and 70s of booze, drugs and wild living was quite frightening, yet it is a mark of his character that he has put all that behind him and now lives a relatively quiet country life with his wife and family.

One particular season we seemed to have a surfeit of admirals of the navy, due mainly to the fact that one of our regular rods was an admiral who during the season would invite his friends to fish and these friends were usually other admirals.

I remember one particular morning meeting the admiral and his guests on the car park, when another rod arrived who happened to be a naval commander, so that day we had a full complement of navy people fishing. As we walked down to the river, the commander jokingly ordered me to go ahead and stand on the footbridge and pipe the admirals aboard! I duly obliged as I had my dog whistles on a cord around my neck and used one of them in obeisance of the command! Not knowing the correct pipe, I made one up, much to the amusement of the assembled company who all saluted in traditional navel style as they marched off down the river bank, and the senior admiral looked back and said to me, "Very good, carry on bosun... full ahead both!"

During the late 90s, a television production company was given permission to use a part of the river to film a few minutes footage for the well-known TV program *Kavanagh QC* in which that well-known actor the late and much-missed John Thaw portrayed the part of Kavanagh. It took two days to capture the required two minutes of filming. The top fields were packed with trucks and lorries as a small transient self-sustaining village sprung up overnight: wardrobe units, lorries loaded with props, actors' caravans and fully equipped mobile kitchens which fed a crew of about fifty people three superb meals each day. To estimate the costs of the whole operation just to film two minutes was difficult to judge, but it is little wonder our TV licenses are so expensive! The village was transformed for a day with one of the cottages beside the river suddenly turned into a quaint riverside pub that even dispensed real beer!

However, the one and only barrel supplied by the props department didn't last very long once the film crew had a chance to taste the local ale during lunch breaks!

Between shots, I noticed John Thaw standing on the footbridge studiously considering the river. On enquiring whether I could help him he said that where he lived there was a small stream flowing through his land and he has been fascinated with all the various water plants that grow in and around his little stream. Unfortunately, he said that he had not the time to find out the names of all the plants, but he did so much appreciate their natural beauty. Before being called for the next shot I spent a very pleasant few minutes identifying for him all the different plants that were in view from the river bridge.

Another shot was of one of the actors stood in the river fly fishing and the shot was to be John Thaw standing on the footbridge talking to this 'fly fisherman'. I had been contracted for the day by the film company to ensure that this 'fly fisherman' looked the part. He had to be dressed correctly to look like a true fly fisherman with all the right fishing clothes, including hat, waders, rod, reel, and line with flies attached. In fact, I was instructed to spend an hour or so teaching the actor, who had never held a fishing rod in his hand before, how to cast with a fly fishing rod! Not an easy task! However, the film director was satisfied with the actor's newly acquired casting skills even if the instructor was not!

The wide diversity of the people who came to fish and do fish the river regularly is amply illustrated by one of the tenants of the fishery who lives in New York and now regularly comes over to fish the Itchen. His occupation until he retired recently was as Conservator of American Art at the Metropolitan Museum in New York. This gentleman would visit with his wife several times during the season and we soon became very good friends, particularly after he had been introduced to the residential hospitality of the Wykeham Arms in Winchester, where they stayed, and the delights of the good lunchtime food and quality wine at the Chestnut Horse. In fact, during one of their visits to the UK they both came all the way up to Scotland to visit my wife and me after I had retired, just to assure themselves that we were both happy in our new home. People are so kind.

The two common threads that link all these reminiscences are fly fishing and the River Itchen. It is interesting to observe that whenever two fly fishers meet for the first time, irrespective of who or what they are, especially along a chalk stream river bank with fly rods in hand, any remaining social class structures that still exist in this country today just seem to melt away. This maybe is what makes fly fishing such a wonderful sport that is enjoyed by such a wide spectrum of the human race.

CHAPTER 40

FLY FISHING RODS OF TODAY

It is indisputable that the majority of fly rods that were on show at the recent Game Fair along the tented lines of Fisherman's Village were of 'Far Eastern' manufacture. However, there were of course good examples of quality 'Western' rods. Although the House of Hardy may now have many of their rods manufactured in the Far East, it is suggested that these rods are manufactured in the Far East to the exact design and quality material criteria that is rigidly set down by Hardy's at Alnwick. In today's cost-conscious world, having rod blanks made from manmade quality-controlled materials in the Far East, where labour costs and material cost are far more advantageous than in the UK, makes sound economic sense. Gone are the days when split cane ruled the roost, where each rod was individually handmade by an expert skilled craftsman and mass production was unheard of! Today's synthetic materials now used to build modern fly rods are all manmade and so the same precise controls and build consistency can be applied to produce one rod blank or 1000 identical rod blanks.

The market in the UK is flooded with many new ranges of fly rods from the lowest price bracket through to the more expensive. Many of these ranges originate from Far Eastern manufacture. After testing many of them it will be found that the majority are quite 'fishable', yet most do not have that important significant 'feel' that Way Yin mentions. They are all very similar in feel and usually exhibit an over-stiff action with few, if any, exhibiting any real 'life' or character that more experienced anglers look for in a quality fly rod. These new ranges of rods may be attractive and acceptable to the average fly fisher who does not know, understand or even care as long as the rod works for him and it is within his price range.

However, it is not until a knowledgeable experienced fly fisher and caster has significant input into the design specification of each specific model of rod that the real differences come to light. This professional experienced input into the design and construction of a rod is essential if the significant requirement for 'feel' and top-quality casting performance is to be achieved when comparisons are made between the cheaper and more expensively designed rods.

The higher the technical input into the design and production of a rod, the better the end product. Generally speaking, it will be found that all the recognised premier rod builders have one or several very experienced fly fishers and top-notch casters and instructors on their design staff. No rod company worth its salt would or should dream of purchasing in bulk or putting their name on rod blanks that they have not had specifically manufactured to their own precise design criteria. It is interesting to note that few of these companies who have introduced new name ranges of rods actually employ any recognised technical expertise in rod design and build. They may employ experienced casters etc. to sell their product but not to design. Cosmetically beautifully finished some of these rods may be; however, the blank is usually from a bog-standard bulk manufacture and purchase and usually originate from somewhere east of the Suez Canal!

Although the retail price of some top of the range rods are over the top in the UK when compared with a similar rod in USA, it is appreciated that much of these costs are in the design and import duties, and that good technical design, including pre-production testing, is time consuming and therefore expensive!

There may well be in the future even cheaper ranges of rods appearing on the market in the UK, but experience demonstrates this has happened before with the initial introduction of glass fibre and carbon fibre. However, time and Darwin's 'survival of the fittest' principle will eventually see many of them disappear. Progressive quality design and build will always win out in the end.

However, the general standards of rods available today within these new era ranges of rods are far better now if compared with similar ranges of rods of 30 years ago when glass and carbon fibre first appeared. A good analogy is the modern Japanese electronics industry. Fifty years ago, Japanese electronic gadgets and gismos were generally copies of quality European goods and initially build standards were unreliable, but as time passed, and with cheap labour, the manufacture and design quality improved until they have now become market leaders worldwide. The same is suggested will apply to Asian fishing rods. So, to promote and improve the standards of manufacture, design and use of fly fishing rods from Asia, what about someone setting up a Spey casting school on the upper River Ganges in India for Mahseer or a casting school on the Yellow River in China for mud fish!

The demand for top quality rods in the UK will at least remain at the present level, but competition for sales will increase. Buying and using a top-quality rod is a subjective decision made by the angler. Therefore, as long as the technical quality, design and performance of these top rod manufacturers continues to regularly improve, then there will always be a steady market for the latest top of the range model(s) in the UK. The latest model of top quality rod either single or two hand is a 'must have' for many fly fishers in the UK.

It is interesting to note that several of the top Western rod makers have introduced into their range 'Entry Level' and 'Middle of the road' rods at sensible prices. These rods have been specifically designed and manufactured to do a good job and anglers are taking to them because many now offer such excellent value. Experience teaches that mediocrity in design standards of fly rods will not prevail in the UK market; even if the national economy goes 'tits up', UK fly fishers will still, most times, find the money for what they really want.

DO CARBON FIBRE RODS SLOW DOWN WITH USE AND AGE? IF SO, IS IT SIGNIFICANT?

THE LONG ANSWER

Historically this was not an uncommon phenomenon experienced in well-used fibreglass blanks. The initial stiffness eroded due to lower fatigue strengths of the composite materials due to 2 primary factors:

1. The woven fiberglass fabrics inherently have multidirectional fibre orientations which are not aligned straight. In a weave, yarns are bent as they cross over and under alternating yarns at various angles. When loaded, non-linear fibres tend to straighten and have to move an extra distance compared to a fibre that is positioned straight from the onset. This puts an extra load on the fibre-resin bond.

2. Early prefinished (the chemical link between the glass fibre and the prepreg resin) and resin systems had lower bond strengths compared to the resins used today.

Materials and designs used in Sage blanks, for example, have extremely high fatigue strengths and will not 'soften' or lose their properties with extended use. This is due to:

1. Selection and use of high performance-high strength quality graphite fibres that have excellent mechanical and resin bonding properties (not all graphite fibres are equal in this area).

2. Sage's exclusive resin system was developed to optimize the resin-fibre bond with high mechanical strengths. Our resin performance far exceeds typical sport grade resin systems.

3. Blank designs and material lay-up techniques that optimize fibre positioning. The fibres are oriented as straight as possible in the direction of the load. This maximizes strength and reduces strain on the resin-fibre bond.

THE SHORT ANSWER

Today's modern carbon epoxy rods have outstanding mechanical and fatigue strengths that far surpass the loads they will experience in a lifetime of use. Because of this their stiffness (action) should be maintained and will not soften over time.

THE SHORTEST ANSWER

No.

CHAPTER 41

PRECAUTIONARY METHODS USED TO PRODUCE STOCKING BROWN TROUT THAT RETAIN A HIGH LEVEL OF GENETIC INTEGRITY

The objective of this project was to produce about 5000 quality stock brown trout of a good genetic status annually for restocking areas of the lower River Itchen where natural reproduction was not strong due to poor spawning conditions. At least this would maintain a reasonable head of catchable trout that were of the right genetic stock for the Itchen. Prior to this, these areas were regularly stocked from various doubtful sources of interbred highly domesticated mixed stocks obtained from commercial hatcheries from far and near, just to maintain a viable commercial put and take river fishery. Although historic reproduction was poor in these areas, this project was backed up with a program of restoration and improvement of these degraded spawning areas. So at least if any natural spawning did occur by any of the sexually mature trout that were left at the end of the fishing season, they would be at least of the right genetic Itchen type fish.

To produce 5000 two plus trout that were, in my opinion, as near as possible of the right genetic status, I developed the following process using my instincts and knowledge gleaned from observing and learning about the wild brown trout in its natural environment:

1. Net out of the upper river, where no stocking has been done for sixty

years, several mixed ages yet mature wild trout both male and female as the initial brood stock.

2. Strip the females (50) for eggs into big containers. Mature wild trout produce 800-1000 eggs per pound body weight.

3. 12 ripe males used to fertilize all the eggs (ratio of one cock fish to every four females approx.).

4. These eggs were then put down in incubators for subsequent hatching all on natural spring and river water.

5. The males once used were returned to the river.

6. Normal hatchery procedures were then followed until fish were two plus (12"-15").

7. This stock was then sold on in spring of third year for stocking, but 30 eyeball selected females were kept back and reared on in ponds as brood females who matured in the fall of same year (at three years old).

8. These females were stripped and the eggs fertilized with milt from fresh wild males netted from the river. At no time were captive males used.

9. The spent females were either killed or sold on as large stock fish and no female was used for eggs more than once.

10. This process once established was replicated year after year.

Yes, there were all the usual problems one faces when rearing trout in a hatchery (fungus, etc.), but with common sense and good hatchery practice most of these can be overcome.

To produce good-looking quality trout it is essential that the fish have sufficient space in which they are reared and are fed correctly in earth ponds with gravel beds with plenty of quality water flowing through.

My objective was to produce quality trout that not only looked good but were as near as I could get of the right genetic status as were the wild trout of the upper river.

To me, the way I operated this project in the 70s and 80s was from just common sense. In those days I had little or no idea what genetic integrity really meant! What goaded me on was that I was convinced then that the stock fish being used to stock some of the chalk streams were of very poor quality, both in looks as well as in their breeding background.

Maybe this artificial rearing process did, or may have, some genetic impact? One thing I am reasonably sure of is that in using this process I was able to produce far more fish of 12"- 15" into the river system than nature could produce from the same number of wild females. Maybe that's one of the flaws in this process! I reduced the natural selection, but who knows and how can one tell? That is briefly it!

CHAPTER 42

LITTLE GREBES (DABCHICKS)

I doubt if there are any regular chalk stream fishermen around that have not, at some time in their fishing experiences, cast to a dabchick 'rise'. So many times I have heard a fisherman tell me how he spent a good half an hour casting to a spot where he claimed he had seen a huge wild trout rise. Usually these huge 'rises' would be seen tight in under the bank from where the fisherman was fishing. The fisherman would have disturbed a skulking dabchick from the thick bank side vegetation which was usually where the hen dabchick had built its waterlogged nest. Yes, I can vouch to the fact that dabchick rises have kept some anglers occupied for hours on end!

In all my years as a river keeper on the Itchen, there would be hardly a season pass when I had not seen dead dabchicks floating down the river. Not that anyone had killed them, nor had any fisherman shot one after he had discovered that he had been casting for hours to a dabchick rise! The culprit of the demise of these dabchicks were bullheads. These little fish are very common in the chalk streams and, in fact, in biomass terms they are the biggest contributor to the total fish biomass of the entire river, believe it or not!

Bullheads are not very big - 3 to 4 inches is a big one. They have a big flattened head and very prickly fins which only hinge one way: backwards. So, if a dabchick catches one – they do feed on them regularly and most times are able to swallow them head first in one gulp – and it is a big bull head and the bird is unable to swallow it in one swallow, it will try to spit the fish out to get rid of it; unfortunately, the spines on the dorsal fin of the bullhead only bend backwards so get immovably impaled into the soft parts of the bird's mouth and throat and the poor bird chokes itself to death.

On the odd occasion I have seen a distressed dabchick floating down the river on its back with its lobed feet pathetically waving in the air, I have managed to fish it out and remove the offending bullhead and then release the bird back to the river. Most times the bird is already dead, so I let nature take its course.

CHAPTER 43

THOUGHTS ON CATCH AND RELEASE OF STOCKED TROUT

Catch and release has long been recognised over the years by fishery managers who work with wild trout as a useful fishery management tool that can be used to protect a particular population of wild or native trout, or a fragile age group of fish within a population, from overexploitation. In trout waters these populations are normally either wild trout or native trout that are or have been overexploited by overfishing, or there have been some environmental problems that have reduced the natural population densities. Only once the environmental problems have been sorted out should a properly implemented catch and release policy be introduced which will over time allow the natural trout population to recover sufficiently, whereby an annual crop can eventually be harvested. In circumstances as such, a catch and release policy can reap substantial benefits.

That is the good news; now for the not so good news! It is hard to find any positive benefits of a catch and release policy on a fishery that relies on regularly planting out catchable-sized hatchery-reared stock trout to sustain a commercial rod letting fishery. This is amply illustrated by some recently reported unfortunate experiences by an angler when fishing one of the classic chalk streams of Hampshire, when he noticed distressed and dying trout floating down from the beats above. One is led to ask how many more trout died that day alone, besides during the whole season on that beat, as every trout that dies does not always float off downstream! There is little doubt in my mind that these distressed and dying trout would have been stocked fish that had been recently caught and released. Whatever care is or had been taken by the anglers above when handling these fish, the stresses imposed on these stock fish by hooking, playing and then releasing were such that they succumbed to those stresses. A classic case, in my opinion, of the last straw that broke the camel's back! This is a statement that requires some explanation.

It first must be clearly understood that all stress in fish is cumulative. A stock trout is under stress from the day it is hatched in the hatchery and throughout every life stage from alevin, swim up fry, to par, to fingerling, right up to the time they are of the required size to be ferried to the river and released. From alevins to release size, these hatchery trout are reared in unnatural conditions, all of which impart stress upon the trout. Furthermore, to compound these stresses the trout are, during their lifetime in the hatchery, regularly netted up and graded and handled and sorted while all mal-forms and finless wonders are culled out. These regular hatchery procedures are essential if quality trout suitable for stocking are to be produced. The stresses imparted to these fish during all these unnatural actions continues to build up throughout their lives in the hatchery ponds. Whereas with wild and native trout, they naturally fend for themselves individually throughout their entire life in the wild and have genetically adapted over many generations to cope and survive successfully within the unique environmental conditions where they were born and grow to maturity totally unaided and unaffected by man.

To utilise catch and release on hatchery-reared fish after they have been stocked out, particularly if water temperatures are high and oxygen levels are low, can seriously affect stocked fish. So when these stock fish are caught and released and appear to swim off quite well at the time, many of these fish weakened through the exhaustion of being hooked and played and the effects of all the accumulated hatchery stress, morbidity sets in and they drift downstream with the current, subsequently to die some hours or even days later in some back eddy or deep pool or clump of weed, where their bodies decompose unseen.

I am very much of the opinion that catch and release on all forms of stock fish should not be used in any circumstance, as it can and does inflict untold damage to stocked trout. Any catch and release policy on stocked trout I suggest should be replaced by a simple daily kill bag limit of say two brace (four trout) or – a less attractive policy for those anglers who want to catch more fish per visit – a kill charge imposed where a set charge is made on every fish killed with no fish returned to the water. I am sure most sporting anglers would be quite satisfied with catching, killing and taking home four good-sized stocked trout at the end of the day.

Furthermore, the commercial fishing pressures of today, particularly on our chalk streams, is now far higher than it was when I first started as a river keeper some fifty years ago. Commercial put and take trout fishing is widespread and is necessary to sustain today's commercial rod letting world. Unfortunately, at the same time many of the old-world traditions and attitudes to dry fly fishing of yesteryear have and are diminishing rapidly. Therefore, enforced bag kill limits on stocked trout would probably not go down too well with many of today's anglers.

Of course, there will always be exceptions to the rule with catch and release and instances of a particular resilient stocked trout that has been caught and released on several occasions during a season are not unusual.

However, it can be shown when looking at the big picture, the monetary costs of all the unnecessary and avoidable mortalities caused by the use of catch and release on stocked trout far outweighs the supposed commercial benefits of thinking that all stocked trout can be used more than once! Experience and history has taught me that wild and native trout have a far greater chance of survival when caught and released than any stock fish.

CHAPTER 44

FURTHER COMMENTS ON CATCH AND RELEASE: SHOULD BARBED HOOKS BE BANNED?

In my opinion the short answer is NO.

Recent research has shown that with trout there is no significant difference in the levels of hooking mortality between fish taken on a single barbed hook or a single barbless hook. This is providing the removal of the hook is undertaken by an angler experienced in the handling of a fish intended for return, who uses the recognised methods of playing. One plus for barbless hooks is they are easier to remove from the trout's mouth. It has been reported that more post-hooking mortalities occurred using double hooks and treble hooks, but it has been found that mortalities have not been as great as one might think.

Barbed hooks, whether single, double or treble, can be difficult to remove from deep within a trout's mouth or throat, in such cases it is advisable to cut the leader at the hook eye and leave the hook in place so the trout can be returned to the water quickly. It's the excessive playing and poor out-of-water handling of a struggling fish in order to remove a badly embedded hook that increases the levels of hooking mortality. Fish with hooks left in the mouth or throat that have been handled properly and released quickly rarely, if ever, keel over.

In my opinion, any commercial 'put and take' fishery rightly or wrongly contemplating promoting C&R, should insist on only single barbless hooks being used; this reduces the stress levels and hooking mortalities of fish that are badly handled by inexperienced anglers. It is an accepted fact that all reared stock trout are under stress from the day they are born until the day they are caught and all stress in stock trout is cumulative so C&R, along with poor handling techniques, compounds stress levels and can increase mortalities. The use of barbed hooks or barbless hooks should be a seriously considered decision by the professional fishery manager. Use barbed hooks for killing fish, yes, but use barbless for C&R on either stocked or wild trout. The majority of post-hooking mortalities on wild and/or stock fish, in my opinion, are mainly due to inappropriate handling combined with poor water conditions – not whether the hook has barbs or not, although barbless hooks will reduce mortalities in most C&R situations.

CHAPTER 45

THE PERILS OF NON-NATIVE INTRODUCTIONS OF FISH INTO RIVERS

I noted with dismay a report in a recent edition of one of the national game angling magazines that said artificially reared grayling were recently released into a major river in Wales. I am taking for granted that this introduction had been authorised and implemented by the Environment Agency. However, in my opinion, introductions of any species of fish that have never been historically indigenous to the river system flies against all the basic and fundamental biological principles of good fisheries management practice laid down in the Water Framework Directive.

I do, however, appreciate in this case the admirable motives behind these introductions (increased fishing opportunities for anglers), but have to ask: can the river naturally sustain and support this introduction, and what impact will these introductions into these waters have on the natural brown trout population? Have any studies and assessments been done on the potential holding capacity of the water?

To help answer these questions other questions should be first answered. For example, have grayling naturally inhabited the river system at any time since the last ice age? If not, when were they first introduced? If introduced by man at some time in the dim and distant past, are there any impassable natural or manmade obstructions in operation that preclude all fish movements upstream?

History teaches that introductions of grayling into a river that historically had no grayling can and does have significant impacts on the resident wild trout populations. A river can only naturally support x-kilos of fish flesh per hectare. Grayling are very good at reproduction if water conditions, habitat and food availability are sufficient, but where the natural resources already sustain a healthy wild trout population it is suggested that the trout population is being sustained to its maximum natural production level, controlled by the present food and habitat availability. To introduce grayling on top of this resident trout population can only put excessive pressure on the natural resident trout. Something somewhere has to give to accommodate the introductions.

Experience teaches that after the initial inevitable population explosion of the grayling has settled down after a couple of seasons, the composition of the original fish biomass before introduction alters significantly. Where the original biomass consisted of almost 100% wild brown trout, and possibly in this case migratory sea trout and young pre-smolt salmon, the change after grayling introduction will be in the range of 65% grayling 35% brown trout, including young sea trout and pre-smolt salmon.

Although the actual fish biomass remains basically static, controlled by food availability, there is a significant reduction in the wild trout population and the young sea trout and pre-smolt salmon. Over time, the actual combined cropped weight of fish caught by the angler (i.e. trout and grayling) will probably remain the same as it was before the grayling were introduced.

Unfortunately, experience again has taught us that once grayling have been introduced into a healthy system it is virtually impossible to eradicate them!

Finally, grayling en masse do have the propensity to move long distances, particularly after spawning in large spate river systems, and that movement is usually downstream to find temporary deeper habitat in which to recover from spawning.

There are few, if any, recognised records that demonstrate that the introduction of a non-native species of fish into a river system has improved fishing opportunities. Most instances have only recorded non-native introductions having negative impacts on a fishery.

If only all the time and money spent on these non-native introductions were spent on the protection, restoration and enhancement of the natural habitat of these rivers and nature left alone to determine the biomass levels of the resident indigenous fish species, the better our fishing would be!

CHAPTER 46

A BRIEF DESCRIPTION OF THE ITCHEN

Having spent 32 years as a river keeper on the River Itchen, many fly fishermen who have never had the opportunity to fish this superb chalk stream and who may have read about the river, often ask me questions about the river. A definitive book could be written about the history and evolution of the River Itchen, and maybe sometime in the future someone will attempt to produce one. Until such time, I will very briefly try to describe through my eyes this wonderful unique river upon which I was privileged to work for all those years.

The River Itchen is recognised as one of the best, if not *the* best, examples of a classic chalk stream that there is in the UK or, in fact, the world. It is a small river of some 32 miles in length from top to bottom, but within it lie some of the best fly fishing beats to be found anywhere.

From within its waters and along its banks, many of the doyens within the history of fly fishing have given us an insight into all that is best in fly fishing. It was at Abbots Barton where G.E.M. Skues spent 56 seasons fishing for brown trout. It was from his experiences and astute observations which he made there which are now recorded in his many classic books, including his accounts on the evolution of nymph fishing as we know it today. Frederick Halford, who is more associated with the neighbouring River Test and was the leading instigator of the dry fly revolution, also leased fishing on the river downstream from Winchester.

There are a host of expert dry fly fisherman who have cut their teeth and spent a great proportion of their fishing lives along the banks of this chalk stream. Sir Edward Grey wrote his famous book *fly Fishing* based on the River Itchen. The legendary Dermot Wilson fished the upper Itchen all his life. The list of names is endless.

The unique characteristics of the river have been maintained, along with astute and informed management and river keeping, and although the volumes of natural fly hatches are now not so intense as they were 30 years ago, dry fly fishing is still the easiest method of catching trout. Wild trout and introduced grayling still abound on the headwaters from Kingsworthy upstream, and sensitive stocking programs maintain quality dry fly fishing for trout and grayling from Winchester downstream, with two productive salmon beats above the tide in Southampton.

Access to quality dry fly fishing is restricted and is usually organised by the respective owners, although day ticket access to quality fishing can be obtained from 'The Rod Box' tackle shop at Kingsworthy. The famous still water trout fishery at Avington Lakes affords excellent stalking for quality stocked rainbows in the gin clear spring waters of the upper Itchen Valley. Day tickets are available, but it is recommended that a phone call would assure the angler of a ticket.

The traditional chalk stream dry fly patterns still rule the roost on the waters of the Itchen and size 18s and 20s of medium olive, iron blue, and blue-winged olive duns and spent patterns of these, along with some size 16 sedge flies, will be sufficient for most days on the river. With of course a selection of pheasant tail nymphs for when the trout are seen to be feeding just below the surface.

As wading is generally not allowed on most beats and the water being gin clear, most fish can be spotted before one casts to them as they lie amongst the heavy tresses of swaying *Ranunculus*. So, astute and clever field craft and accurate casting is essential if any sport is to be expected.

The Itchen dry fly fishing is about the best it gets... anywhere! But there again I am somewhat biased, I suppose.

CHAPTER 47

THE RIVER TEST

Having written a brief description of the River Itchen, I feel to avoid any obvious bias I have towards the Itchen I should now describe briefly the great River Test.

If the River Itchen in Hampshire is regarded as the queen of chalk streams, then the River Test arguably must therefore be the king.

It was along the banks of this wonderful fertile chalk stream that held such a variety of insect life that dry fly fishing evolved and became recognised as a most thrilling way to catch rising trout. Through the 1800s and well into the 1900s notable anglers cut their teeth on this river as they honed their expertise and developed the use of the dry fly. None more so than Frederic Halford who for so many years fished the river and leased some of many now historical beats that provided him with the knowledge and information that he recorded within his writings. Halford promoted through his writing a chalk stream ethic of 'upstream dry fly only to a rising fish'. This mantra established by him so many years ago and rigidly adopted by many fisheries and upheld since by generations of fly fisher folk on the chalk streams, is now fortunately being softened by a more realistic attitude to dry fly fishing by many of today's fly fishers.

Unfortunately, like many other rivers in the UK, the Test is also suffering from a reduction in the volume of the natural aquatic insects that have sustained the sport of dry fly fishing over the years. Although many substantial trout are still taken on the dry fly, particularly during mayfly time and where dry fly-only rules apply, these changing conditions have tended to increase the use of heavier nymphs, and subsurface lures and attractors are now increasingly being used.

Access to quality fishing on this hallowed river which for so long was mainly only available to an exclusive few is now more readily available as owners now open up more opportunities for visitors to test their skills on these historic waters. With good winter rainfalls the chalk streams are virtually assured of good water flows for most of the summer.

To many fly fishermen, even to walk the banks of these hallowed waters can be quite daunting, let alone fish these wonderful rivers. All one really needs is a 9ft four or five weight rod with double taper line, a 12-foot leader down to 5x tippet and a selection of traditional chalk stream dry flies, 16s, 18s, and 20s, plus a few pheasant tail nymphs and a selection of sedge flies. With this selection one would expect to have some serious dry fly fishing action for some magnificent brown trout and quality rainbows.

Although not cheap, but comparable to some of the still water fisheries in Hampshire, fishing time can be arranged on some quality historic waters of the Test by contacting either an individual owner or one of the following letting agents:

The Rod Box, Kingsworthy, Winchester, Hants.
Famous Fishing, e-mail: enquiries@famousfishing.co.uk
Robjents, High St, Stockbridge, Hants.

CHAPTER 48

WHY I USE LONG-TAILED DRY FLIES

During the many years spent as a river keeper on the River Itchen, it was my habit to make mental notes of much of what I learnt during those years from my observations of the wonderful natural world that is the insect life of a chalk stream. I did this for not only my own information, instruction and guidance on the ways to fish the dry fly more successfully on the river upon which I was so privileged to work, but more so to pass on information to any willing listeners.

Many of my more significant observations of aquatic insects were made with my nose just 12 inches from the surface of the river! As the height of the river flow seldom fluctuated significantly on the upper Itchen, many of the footbridges crossing the river were rarely built more than 12 inches above the water level. Lying flat on my stomach on the deck of a bridge enabled me to spend many adsorbing hours observing the moving river surface from a mere 8-12 inches. In pursuing this occupation, over time, I learnt to note and recognise almost every item that floated by on or suspended in the surface film. It is not until such lengthy observations have been conducted does one realise the amount and diversity of insect life that actually passes by unseen by an angler on the river bank.

Nature illustrates this very well on any hot, dry and breezy summer's day, as it is astonishing to note the amount and diversity of insects that drift by unnoticed. Many of which dry fly fisherman have yet to imitate, let alone identify and name. These insects consist mainly of terrestrial species made up by a host of tiny spiders and a wide range of minute creepy crawlies with and without wings that have been blown onto the water from the surrounding countryside or have dropped off from overhanging trees and bank side vegetation. However, from these early observations I have since revised somewhat my thoughts on the term 'smutting trout' and what the trout in these circumstances actually may be eating!

Over the course of time I was able to study closely most species of natural insect that dry fly fishers of the chalk streams do recognise. From the early hatches of large dark olive through to the iron blue, mayfly, medium olive, blue-winged olive, pale wateries, etc., including sedges. From ascending nymphs and hatching nymphs to dun and spinner stages, all were closely observed at some time or other whilst lying flat on my stomach on a footbridge. All aided using a homemade shallow muslin scoop net six inches square and a cheap Sherlock Holmes-type magnifying glass.

By observing the natural emerging duns as they floated by, one of the first things that became obvious in the early days was that not all the nymphs hatched out into perfectly formed duns. It was surprising how many did not manage to attain that perfect classic dun profile with two upright wings, fully pumped up with blood and with all their legs in the right position and not penetrating the surface film and with their tails perfectly cocked. So often a single wing or both wings were crumpled or the legs were either entrapped in the surface film, broken or damaged or the thorax inextricably caught up in the nymphal shuck. Whatever the causes, the insect was unable to take flight to complete its life cycle. One thing that caught the eye was that in many cases with a damaged dun its tail was clearly visible on or above the surface film. Experienced dry fly fishers recognise and come to expect to see 'cripples' regularly floating down during a hatch of fly and trout taking them quite readily.

A good imitation or impression of the natural insect is what most traditional dry fly fishers seek to achieve when tying their own dry flies. So, the 64,000-dollar question is what attracts wild trout to readily rise to take crippled naturals which to the human eye appear to bear little resemblance in profile to the classic natural dun? One possible response could be it is movement that is acting as the 'trigger' as the insect struggles to free and right itself. A hypothesis that is difficult to substantiate! Consideration should be given to the fact wild trout do intercept and feed on ascending nymphs and nymphs that are attached to the underside of the surface film and nymphs that are undergoing the emerging stage. Logically, wild trout must recognise all these stages as food before they even consider taking a dun. So, is there a common 'trigger' factor in each of these early life stages that stimulates wild trout to feed or is all done by trial and error by the trout?

Experience teaches dry fly fishers that feeding wild trout can be very selective in their feeding habits. Wild trout can and will at times concentrate on feeding exclusively on only one of the many stages of an insect's life, even if there is an abundance of the other stages readily available. Furthermore, it is suggested that wild trout can and do have the ability to differentiate between the duns of, for example, a large dark olive, iron blue and a medium olive when all three are hatching at the same time. Experience teaches that wild trout will probably select to take the iron blue first, even if there are only a few hatching and the iron blue duns are far and away outnumbered by the duns of the other two species. However, I digress!

When observing the spinner stage within the life cycle of these insects, the same applied in many cases with 'crippled' spinners. Spinners that fall onto the water, many observed, did not take on the classical spinner pose of two transparent wings spread flat out on the water with the body in place and the tails laying out perfectly behind in the classic spinner position. Having on many an occasion fished the ebbing minutes of an evening rise with a size 18 Lunn's Particular, which is a classical spinner pattern for the medium olive, yet my fly has had one single wing broken off by my poor casting or both wings have fallen off because of my poor fly tying and or/the fly has been chewed up by an eager trout. So often a tattered fly as such which bears no resemblance to its pristine state continued to catch trout. Why is this? The only common factor noticed in these situations was that the stiff micro fibbet long tails of the artificial used were still well in place and very obvious.

This may be attributed to my fly tying method of tying longer tails on my dry flies than those usually recommended by the professional fly tiers of the time. After some thought I started to tie my flies with even longer tails, as I slowly concluded that these extra-long tails could well be acting as the 'trigger factor' that attracted trout to take the artificial concoction that was my fly. Particularly when the rest of the fly bore little resemblance to the profile of a natural fly or any recognised artificial pattern.

There has been discussion of late on 'trigger factors', particularly within dry fly fishing circles, over what exactly constitutes the incorporation of a 'trigger factor' when designing and tying dry flies. Experience gained by mainly using extra-long tailed flies has suggested to me that my catches of trout over the years may not have been as successful if I had used nothing else but shop-bought short tailed flies, but there again who knows as I have rarely bought or used shop tied dry flies. If anything, during my latter years I tied in even longer tails to further exaggerate what, in my opinion, was the 'trigger factor'. These patterns, as illustrated along with others, have worked well for me over the years, but doubtless there are many who would prefer to adopt different ideas on 'trigger factors' that can be shown to be equally as productive.

It should be clearly understood that all the observations made and described have been on wild brown trout. The observed feeding preferences of recently stocked brown trout can and do differ from those of resident wild brown trout, but that is another can of worms!

Every angler is entitled to consider that their own ways and methods are best, so long as they can catch fish with them. Confidence in using a particular pattern of fly and in the way it is tied and expertly presented to the quarry are all paramount to the dry fly fisher. These among the many are the wonderful charms of dry fly fishing. They present opportunities for further observation of the natural world in our efforts to resolve the many challenges which nature presents and opens up endless fields for discussion and speculation all of which hopefully stimulates further experiment.

CHAPTER 49

AQUATIC WEED MANAGEMENT IS THERE A NEED?

Many queries and requests for advice have been received regarding the prolific growths of aquatic weed that have this summer plagued many rivers, ponds, lakes and reservoirs of the British Isles, including some highland rivers, burns and lochs of Scotland this year. Not wishing to blame it all on possible climate change and eutrophication of our aquatic ecosystems, but there has, however, been a series of warm winters each followed by a mild spring that has encouraged many varieties of water weed to grow prolifically from early spring through to late summer. Normally any prolonged frosts during winter increases the severity of winter die-back in most aquatic plants so reducing its strength of growth the following year, but that has not happened for several years.

Not wishing to go into the whole history of weed cutting in rivers except to say that aquatic weed management has been a problem in lowland rivers for centuries and long before river keepers were employed solely to maintain rivers for fisheries purposes. River keepers however were employed three hundred or more years ago, but their remits in those early times were purely to maintain manmade river banks and keep feeder channels and operative mill leats clear of weed to allow water flows into and through mills to run unimpeded. So, it was not until rivers became less industrialised and sporting fisheries interests grew, did the river keepers turn to methods of weed management that would increase and maintain the angling opportunities for their masters. History teaches us that fishing on many lowland streams was, particularly in the early days of fly fishing, only done in early spring through until the annual emergent weed growth became so prolific that any form of angling became almost impossible. In other words, trout fishing with a fly on the chalk streams became difficult after the mayfly had finished sometime in middle to late June. The early records of the famed Houghton Club on the River Test show that mayfly time was the only time of the year the rivers were seriously fished. Nowadays full-time experienced keepers are able to keep the weed under control and underwater by regular cutting each month from April unto October, thus allowing angling to be carried on unimpeded by excessive weed growths for the entire fishing season.

Apart from these lowland chalk streams, in the normal course of events many fishery managers have not had to regularly cope with such prolific weed growths which have occurred this season and therefore they have little experience to draw upon to enable them to deal with it efficiently. It is not until the excessive growth has almost stopped anglers fishing that the complaints from the fishermen start to be made and by then it is usually too late to do much about it. Panicked attempts are usually made to deal with the excess growths, but unless the problem is dealt with by someone who has had good experience and knows how the problem can be tackled efficiently and has the right tools and manpower available, the anglers are seldom satisfied.

There are many species of aquatic weed and excessive growth of any one, or several together, can be a problem and even a danger to a fishery and adjacent land. Too much weed in a river will drastically reduce the living space for fish, so they move off to find space elsewhere. Besides reducing the fishing opportunities for the fisherman, the bed of the river becomes over-shaded, which may affect insect life and its activity. Weed is, however, an essential contributor to the habitat quality of many rivers, lakes and ponds, but it is more efficient if the volumes are well-managed and kept in balance with the rest of the habitat. One of the main and most important concerns over excessive weed growths in rivers is land drainage and flood defence. A river channel so choked with weed will be found to not only reduce the speed of the flow but, by water displacement, it will dramatically raise the water levels which in turn can threaten to flood surrounding land. Incidence of summer flooding of land adjacent to weed-choked waterways has been a common occurrence over the years, particularly when accompanied by a summer thunderstorm.

It's good to remember that in still waters, excessive weed growths can and do de-oxygenate the water and serious fish kills have resulted from such excessive weed growth. This is caused by photosynthesis in water plants which is a natural process that stimulates water plants to pump oxygen into the water during the day. However, the procedure reverses at night when the oxygen is taken back into the plant, thus drastically reducing the oxygen levels throughout the night and reaching the minimum low levels around dawn. This natural process can be exacerbated when it coincides with low water levels, high water temperatures and fluctuating barometric pressures associated with thunderstorms.

Rarely does this occur in running water, although it is quite common for fish life to become very stressed at times even in running water when, again, low flows, high temperatures and heavy weed growths coincide.

How can the excessive weed growth problem be tackled? Initially, where experience is limited, it is vital that each situation is assessed by an individual who has had experience in weed management both in running water and in still water situations. Good advice will then direct the right course of action that should be taken. No two situations are the same, so different remedies and methods may be required. In rivers and lakes, cutting is the usual method used, whereby a sharp two-handed scythe would be used to harvest the excess weed. In still waters it is essential to remove all cut weed, as if allowed to collect into large rafts and left to rot down in the water, then water quality can be compromised. The same applies to rivers, so cut weed must be removed from the water course unless, like the chalk streams in Hampshire, cut weed by prior arrangement is allowed free passage right down to the sea.

Where depths are such that wading and hand cutting with a scythe is impossible in either pond, lakes or rivers, then mechanical methods must be considered with the use of a powered boat fitted with a powered weed cutter. Hand operated chain scythes can be used where mechanical means are unavailable.

It must be remembered that there are three main reasons to cut weed and the order of priority is:
1. To maintain water levels for flood defence and land drainage purposes
2. To increase living space for fish and maintain good fish habitat
3. To maintain and improve fishing access and opportunities for anglers

Other than the mechanical methods mentioned, in still waters and in some slow-flowing lowland rivers, black plastic sheeting securely fixed to the bed and left in position for six months will kill unwanted aquatic weed by shading out light. Furthermore, in ponds that are drainable, reducing the water levels and laying the pond bed open to winter frosts will help control waterweed growth the following season.

Fisheries on rivers that have historically only suffered from excessive weed growths are now finding occasionally, with the milder winters and warmer summers, that weed tends to start to grow earlier in the year and continues right through to Sept/Oct. On the lowland chalk streams, river owners and their keepers have had generations of experience in weed management and have devised cooperative weed cutting programmes for each river system whereby weed is cut by all, each month from April through to Oct at, and on, the same dates in each month. This allows cut weed to free flow direct down to the sea, which saves a great deal of hard work in removing cut weed. However, rivers that have no trained personnel to operate such a programme because they have not been needed in the past, are now increasingly finding weed growths are becoming a problem. The best advice to give is to keep a close eye on the first growth of the season. By this close observation, as soon as the weed begins to grow in the spring, it is wise to give it a good trim, even if it looks OK to the untrained eye. By keeping on top of the growth by regularly trimming every month from April through to October, a suitable pattern can be established and maintained in the growths that gives space for fish as well as providing cover, food and feeding lies for fish. Once the weed can grow too long and thick then the job of cutting becomes very difficult and usually defeats many a willing volunteer worker, particularly where many tonnes of cut weed needs to be removed.

Unless an agreed programme of weed cutting is in place whereby weed is cut each month by all on the same days and the cut weed allowed free passage, then weed removal becomes a problem. To remedy this, temporary weed booms or nets that collect cut weed need to be installed at intervals down the river system that are manned at all times during the cut. Experience teaches us that in a one-man operation with a weed boom or net in place, then one hour's weed cutting requires two hours' hauling out! Finally, a word of warning if large piles of cut weed are left on the river banks to rot down close to the river margin: Serious attention must be paid to ensure the liquids that will drain out of this rotting vegetation does not seep back into the water course, for obvious reasons. Disperse these piles of weed evenly so the vegetation dries out before it disintegrates or remove it from the river bank and disperse over agricultural land.

CHAPTER 50

GRAYLING UNDER THE MICROSCOPE

John Goddard mentions in an article in a recent fishing magazine that on the water he fishes on the Itchen, he has found that the grayling is becoming increasingly more difficult to catch, particularly the larger grayling.

It is suggested that the cause of this phenomenon may not be solely due to the lack of fly, but to the constant unrelenting use of catch and release of the grayling in conjunction with the greatly increased fishing pressure there is now on many of our rivers. On some chalk streams it would not be surprising to find that there is hardly a single day in the season when the trout and grayling do not see an array of artificial flies and nymphs thrown at them. There is little doubt that wild trout and wild grayling do learn quickly to become warier and far less exuberant in their taking habits of surface artificial flies and submerged nymphs when subjected to consistent intensive fishing pressure.

It is an accepted fact that constant fishing pressure and unrelenting catch and release of stocked trout, wild trout, and grayling, increasingly makes the fish more difficult to catch.

History teaches us that before the use of catch and release became a popular management tool and grayling fishing became more popular, grayling was treated as vermin on many classic chalk streams. It is not many years ago when all grayling caught were instantly killed and none returned, irrespective of size. It is little wonder those wild grayling populations of yesteryear remained very naive and comparatively simple to catch. These earlier populations were only allowed to make one mortal mistake in their lives. So, they had no chance to learn from the catch and release experience or be taught to be cautious in the future! Many grayling populations of today are regularly fished over with dry fly and nymph day in and day out for season after season. Many small grayling and even some of the larger ones are caught and released more than once, so there is little doubt they learn from the experience and that the medium to large grayling have now become very difficult to catch.

Similarly, with stocked trout in some smaller still waters where constant catch and release is the rule, these rules soon teach the trout to be wary of anything that moves or even looks like food. It has been shown quite conclusively that heavy fishing pressure and regular catch and release in such situations can eventually stop fish feeding altogether. To such an extent that in some circumstances the trout eventually dies of stress and starvation when, in fact, there is plenty of good natural insect life in the water. (See Alex Berendt, Two Lakes Conference 1980)

John Goddard states in his article that in his opinion the amount of surface insect activity has reduced over recent years on the Itchen, as it has done on other well-known rivers, and I tend to agree with him. Fortunately, the numbers and overall biomass weight and condition of wild fish in the form of grayling in the Itchen still appears to be very healthy, so there must be sufficient subsurface natural food available, considering grayling are predominantly bottom and mid-water feeders.

In my opinion, if fishery owners wish to improve the sporting quality of the grayling fishing on their rivers where grayling are now difficult to catch, a regulated return to a to a total catch and kill policy would soon remedy the perceived problem of uncatchable grayling. Grayling normally breed very successfully in the chalk streams, so the wild stocks would not diminish and would remain in a healthy state. There is a firmly held belief that unrelenting catch and release of grayling and stocked trout on heavily fished chalk streams, albeit being 'the modern thing to be seen to do' these days, is unnecessary and does far more harm than good to the sporting quality of a fishery. Other than that, grayling is great to eat filleted and grilled with a rasher of streaky bacon over the top!

CHAPTER 51

CHALKSTREAM REHABILITATION: IS THERE A NEED?

Having been born in the heart of the Hampshire chalk stream valleys and subsequently working professionally as a river keeper on the upper River Itchen for thirty years, I have made it my duty during that time to attain a good working knowledge of this wonderful chalk stream river. Understanding how and when the river was first made naturally and then particularly how man has continually altered it since the retreat of the last ice age, and how it has arrived in the physical state it is now found in today, is essential knowledge if the question of "Chalk stream rehabilitation: is there a need?" can be answered.

If it is considered that 'to rehabilitate' is to restore to a former state, or to make fit again, or reinstate conditions, then serious thought has to be given to whether the River Itchen needs to be, or should be, rehabilitated.

History informs us that the River Itchen is a totally manmade multichannel system from its several sources down to the sea. Man, specifically from the Bronze and Iron age onwards, has steadily continued over the last 3000 years to develop this water system for his own many and different requirements. The first changes came from the early clearances of the forested downlands to make room for livestock. This was followed by the clearing, in-filling and draining of the heavily vegetated oozing bog that once covered the entire flood plain. Next came the creation of the many high and low cut channels that created heads of water to power the many water mills and for use by the floated meadow drowning systems. In their heyday there would have been one operative water mill on every mile of river, thirty-two in total. All these manmade influences have left today's river keepers a legacy that is an aquatic ecosystem that is structurally and predominantly very artificial. There is confidence in stating that throughout the entire Itchen system there is little or no river bank or river channel that has not been man-created at some point.

After taking all the history into consideration and before an attempt to answer the question of whether 'rehabilitation' is necessary, it may be wise to take a closer look at the present status of the aquatic ecosystem that is the River Itchen system from a fishery's point of view.

The water quality generally throughout the system is excellent with a majority of sampling sites giving constant A1 readings. Ninety nine percent of the mean base flows are maintained by natural springs. Abstraction being almost fully compensated by the return of quality treated effluent and by use of the groundwater pumping compensation schemes on the Candover Brook and River Alre in times of extremely low flow. Fishery management objectives throughout the length of the river are primarily concentrated on salmonid species with the coarse fish species given a very low profile.

Historically the lower reaches of the river, including the three salmon beats, and middle reaches up to Abbotsworthy, have relied upon regular heavy stocking to maintain them as viable sporting trout fisheries. With good habitat management and control of angling pressure, most of the upper reaches have been able to maintain the world famous self-sustaining stocks of wild brown trout.

The only reason this status quo has been maintained for so long is because the fishery owners have wanted it this way. For the past 200 years and more, they have maintained the river system as a mixed salmonid fishery albeit a semi-artificial one. To achieve this objective, they have employed substantial numbers of full-time river keepers to protect, enhance, create and restore where necessary the suitable salmonid habitats. These river keepers have also controlled other species of fish that were deemed to be 'in the way'.

Historically, individual fishery owners have decided the fishery management policies for their own waters. At times some of these policies have scarcely been conducive to good catchment and fisheries practice. The Test and Itchen Association (T&I), now part of the newly formed Wessex Chalk Stream Rivers Trust, influence some owners. Although the Trust has no legal clout, it does try to do a good job and has the voluntary support of most of the major river owners within the catchment area. The Environment Agency and English Nature are in stronger positions legally. Even so, they can rarely influence the objectives of individual riparian owners determined to maintain their waters as salmonid fisheries, wild or stocked.

The attitudes and objectives of the 'agencies' have changed recently with a definite move away from maintaining, at all costs, artificial salmonid fisheries and in their policies towards using stock fish to maintain viable fisheries.

Furthermore, the radical change in policies by certain wildlife trusts towards fishery management may have created a dangerous precedent throughout the world of fisheries management – not only on the chalk streams but countrywide. This has been highlighted by the well-publicised change in policy direction that occurred a few years ago at the very historic Abbots Barton fishery on the River Itchen, where the local wildlife trust has imposed certain regulations on the river beat it owns that could very well drastically alter the habitat for trout and other wildlife, where that habitat has been diligently nurtured and successfully maintained for brown trout and the attendant wildlife by the fishery managers for the past 150 years or more.

The introduction by the wildlife trust of the policy of 'benign neglect' could, in time, alter the habitat that has been maintained for so long for brown trout and wildlife into a habitat that sustains a totally different range of flora and fauna. Of course, it must be understood and accepted that this is just nature working and trying its hardest to adapt to a change in management policy. Now the river is endeavouring to return itself to its former original pristine state using only the very limited natural elements that man has left at this site. This is after man has inflicted upon it all the many changes over the centuries, like dredging and channel re-alignment and flood plain draining etc. Unfortunately, this area is a perfect example of a totally manmade chalk river system. This is illustrated by the high and low cut carriers and manmade flood meadows that lie adjacent to a heavily canalised and dredged and straightened mainstem. All of which, if left untended, will weed up, silt up and grow in with some of the more undesirable species of non-indigenous vegetation. 'Benign neglect' is a very useful rehabilitation tool when used sensibly, and in the right place it can be shown to have great benefits. However, there is a view that in this circumstance its use may be a very retrograde step and could well have serious long-term ecological effects on the adjacent waters. In time it may also have negative impacts on the overall health and wealth of the flora and fauna of whole River Itchen system. As in any aquatic ecosystem such as the Itchen, everything is interconnected. However, as this has changed with a revision of the wildlife trust's policies, the management of Abbots Barton water has now returned to a more sustainable level, whereby the river will be managed in a more environmentally sustainable manner, whereby fly fishing will return to these waters under the auspices of the Piscatorial Society after all the necessary restoration measures have been taken.

It will be very difficult to answer the original question because many other decisions have also to be made beforehand and these will direct the final answer. So what decisions have to be made? There has to be, firstly, a conservation management policy that positively produces rather than just negatively protects.

If the Itchen is to survive in the present state as many require, it has be understood and agreed that the entire aquatic ecosystem that is the River Itchen and its catchment has to be managed as one complete ecological unit. Once this principal is agreed, the use of a fully integrated catchment management plan that sets out the overall and agreed objectives for the whole system is then required. Until this is achieved it will not be possible to pinpoint where and what rehabilitation needs to be done. This new paradigm will identify if there is the need for rehabilitation.

It is unrealistic and unfeasible to expect or even to try to return the river system back to its historic natural pristine state that existed before the first man stepped into the valley. Therefore, serious thought has to be directed as to what state is required and how that can be achieved utilising the few remaining natural elements that enables it to be maintained economically in the future. The answers to these and more immediate questions and concerns may lie in the forthcoming European Legislation enshrined in the five main points of the 'Water Framework Directive'. However, serious concern is being voiced about the ability of the relative agencies and in particular their local advisors to fully interpret all the five salient objectives of this legislation prior to its implementation. The 'Water Framework Directive' gives the whole community a 'one off' opportunity to ensure that our rivers and their entire catchments are managed as one complete aquatic ecosystem. Anything less, it is suggested, could well spell disaster for the long-time future protection and maintenance of our rivers and their catchments.

There is a consensus of opinion that believes the River Itchen is now in better overall health than it has been for some centuries. This state, albeit being a very artificial manmade aquatic system and despite the substantial threats of some present-day problems, has to be sensitively managed, regularly maintained and protected.

With the use of good fisheries science and the other branches of rivers and Earth sciences that are now available and, more importantly, given there is a common will throughout the local communities, and with various river users and land owners within the catchment, the future quality of this very artificial river system could be secure. Good science and a sensitive use of nature's own regeneration powers will guide present and future generations to produce and maintain economically and environmentally sustainable aquatic ecosystems. It requires the sustainable use of what is left of the natural elements remaining and that includes self-sustaining fish populations (albeit limited) which thrive naturally within the system.

History informs us that these chalk streams were not in the past all that productive at times regarding salmonids but were, at their best, just average dual-purpose fisheries and then only when water quality allowed. Species diversity was rather poor even in the 'good old days' before man laid his grubby little fingers upon it! The salmonids have only flourished well as and when man intensively tended the river for them.

The river will naturally continue to try its hardest to return itself to its former state, whether it is left alone or not. However, with the many manmade changes made over the centuries that have at times been extremely radical, this former pristine state is now quite an unrealistic objective for man to even attempt to regain. To allow or encourage the river to try unaided in its present highly changed state is deemed by some to be a foolhardy exercise and very short-sighted if the river system is ever to retain any social value or exhibit natural beauty to humans.

Conservation of the aquatic ecosystem in these urbanising valleys has to positively produce rather than just negatively protect for some hypothetical biological reasons only. All required forms of wildlife and flora will prosper provided the right seeds are supplied and the right habitat is provided and that the 'big picture' of the entire river and catchment is included in the decision making.

A great deal depends on the outcome of the necessary decision making that has to be undertaken. Only after the right decisions have been made will the future of the Itchen and its catchment be secure. The consensus is that if the status quo is required to be maintained, then yes, there is a great deal of work to be done, but until such time the future management strategies of the whole system have been established, the future still appears to be very unsure. Unfortunately, there is also deep concern in some quarters that any agreement to manage the river and catchment as a whole ecological unit may never come about. Therefore, all the best intentions could go by the board and the river will continue to decline and suffer from the impacts of a wide diversification of ideas on how the catchment and river should be managed now and in the years to come. If we do not know where we are going, then any road will get us there.

An illustration of the importance of adopting the catchment perspective can be seen in the problems that face many of the chalk streams today. Problems which may not lie between the river banks but may well be related to the effects of man's land use practices within the catchment. This is manifested in the insidious problem of the possible detrimental effect of diffuse solute pollution and sediments carried into the watercourses from non-point source surface and subsurface runoff. A symptom of these effects is well illustrated in the observed and well-documented slow but regular decline in the volumes of macro invertebrates. The prolificacy of these aquatic and terrestrial insects has historically maintained the great natural wonder and economic value of the historic trout fisheries of this and other beautiful chalk streams. So maybe it is protection that is required and not rehabilitation?

CHAPTER 52

MANMADE RIVERS CAN WORK – A BRIEF HISTORY OF THE RIVER ITCHEN

To finish off this compilation of stories and experiences and personal philosophies, I have put together a brief personally researched history of my favourite river that I was so privileged to have worked upon as a river keeper. I fell in love with the River Itchen from our very first meeting and, just like a treasured secret lover one can never forget, it captured my heart and will unceasingly keep me faithful, fascinated and enthralled for the rest of my life.

IN THE BEGINNING

It was the melting of the great ice fields which covered most of Great Britain at the end of the last ice age ten thousand years ago that chiselled out the valley of the River Itchen and rounded off the surrounding chalk hill to form the topography of the Itchen catchment as we see it today.

As the ice fields retreated, the hills became heavily wooded with oak, elm, yew & holly and the flood plains filled with willow, alder, reed, carr & sedge. If I can take you back to the flood plain of the Itchen, this is what we could have expected to see throughout the valley floor some four thousand years ago. Although Stone Age man wandered the high ground as hunter gatherers seven thousand years ago, it was not until around three thousand years ago that Bronze Age man arrived and settled on the drier higher ground that surrounds the Itchen valley. As they cleared the hills of woodland for firewood and to create space for their primitive forms of agriculture which included the needs of their animals, they also created tracks from their homes on the hillside down to the wet flood plains to enable them to collect water for themselves and to water their stock. These tracks are still used today, though not for the same purposes, and at the top of each of these lanes traces of Bronze Age and later Iron Age settlements can still be found.

At that time, the Itchen valley floor was just an oozing bog and the flood plain as we know it today was covered with dense growths of willow, alder, reed, carr and sedge etc., and with a myriad of spring-fed but heavily silted streams which seeped their way slowly down towards the sea. Early man soon discovered the unique characteristics of chalk springs, thousands of which bubbled up throughout the length and breadth of the flood plain, with constant flows of quality water at a constant temperature of 10 degrees C. The inhabitants soon noticed that when winter froze and scorched off the grasslands on the hillsides, the water did not freeze in the valley bottom and the lush vegetation which grew lasted almost the year round. To make the most of this, the inhabitants started to clear the valley bottom to construct the green and fertile pastures we see today for their own use and for their stock. The myriad of boggy streams was, in time, channelled into fewer and fewer streams until eventually one or two main channels were formed and, in places, these original channels can still be seen today. In and during the intervening centuries, valley residents have used these manmade channels for many and various purposes. History informs us that the next major influence was the arrival of the Romans in the month of August 55BC and being the clever engineers they were, they used the river water for their own benefit and even today Roman culverts and channels are still in use under and around the ancient city of Venta Belgarum (Winchester). They also constructed water meadows around the city for agricultural use and, again, some of these are still in use today. Following the retreat of the Roman Empire in AD440, the Itchen Valley, like the rest of Great Britain, passed through a period we call the Dark Ages. As the influences of the well-organized Roman civilization retreated, civilized progress in this country almost came to a halt and it is not until the early Middle Ages that we can trace any further major changes in the valley. In the interim period, the Viking, Angles, Jutes & Saxon invasions took place and their influences tended to break up what meagre stable civilization existed, and, except for some Saxon influence, it was not until the Norman Conquest in 1066 that we can see any major forms of civilization returning to the valley.

It was the spread of Christianity and the construction of the original church in Winchester (that eventually became Winchester Cathedral) more than 1000 years ago, when we can really say that civilization as we know it returned to the Itchen valley. It was for the construction of this wonderful building which was built on a bog and, to this day, still floats on a raft of oak logs, that the then Archbishop William of Wykham decreed that as much oak as was needed to build the Cathedral should be felled from his lands on the hills of the upper River Itchen valley and be floated down the river for the use of the builders. This indicates there must have been no obstructions to impede the flows and sufficient water to float huge green oak tree trunks, several miles along the river course.

In 1348 the then Bishop of Winchester, Bishop de Lucy, directed that a dam should be built across the valley at Alresford, some eight miles from the source of the river. It was duly built, and it impounded 200 acres of water, the purpose of which was to create a sufficient head of water which, when released in a controlled manner, would create such a head of water to allow large rafts which were loaded with bales of wool to ride the flood all the way down the river to the town of Southampton, some thirty miles away. The wool was then ferried across the English Channel to supply the growing wool trade with Europe. This dam is still there, although the impoundment is now only about 20 acres, as the pond has silted and grown in over the centuries and is now a nature reserve.

No accurate records of fish or fish life are known during these periods; in fact, I very much doubt if there were many fish species which could survive in some parts of the main river channel - probably only in the headwater streams. This is borne out by an account in the city records of Winchester, when, in 1538, the inhabitants of Lower Brook Street, which still runs parallel and alongside the Itchen as it passes through the lower end of the city, had to be evacuated to Middle and Upper Brook Street higher up the city, as the stench from the river was so great that the inhabitants were unable to tolerate it and cholera was rife.

The next major influence by man on this manmade river, was the construction of water mills from the late 1500s through to the mid-1700s. Grist mills and sawmills were built to an intensity of a mill per mile of the river. The last operative mill was closed just after the last war and those which have not been demolished have now been transformed into desirable living accommodation. It was at the height of this milling era that we see the first river keeper employed. His job then was little to do with fish but to keep the mill heads clear of the prolific aquatic weed growths and to maintain the manmade river banks which created the heads of water to power the mills. This valley was at the centre of the wool trade, with many of these mill heads used to dip and wash sheep and also to wash and dye the shorn wool. Several mills were called Fulling Mill as 'fulling' is a medieval English word for sheep dipping or woof washing. Even in these early times various crude chemicals were used to dye wool and to wash sheep to kill parasites and these would have been detrimental to the fish populations.

It was in the late 1700s and early 1800s that the mills began to fall out of use as the Industrial Revolution grew and the Reform Acts of 1832 took their toll, and life began to change in the Itchen Valley.

Wealthy people whose riches were accrued from the Industrial Revolution began to buy up vast chunks of land that included substantial lengths of the river. It was these wealthy industrialists and merchant bankers, or 'Robber Barons' as they were called locally, who had the money and the time to take their pleasures from within their estates and to partake of the harvest of fish from the river. It was, by this time, that the river had partially recovered from most of the misuses it had suffered over the centuries; just by sheer neglect and non-use by man, the river had cleansed itself and had started to regenerate quite naturally. Though one last agricultural use persisted in places right into the 20th Century and that was the drowning system of the water meadows.

Although most of the mills had ceased operation but were still in place, the river keepers had still to be employed to control aquatic weed growths and to carry out necessary bank maintenance, mainly to protect valuable land and property in the flood plain from summer flooding. It was the evolution of dry fly fishing and the building of the split cane rods which helped to shape the management of the Itchen from this time on and has continued to do so, right through until the dawn of the 21st century. Regular accounts of the sport of fly fishing for fish, and especially brown trout, can be found in the literature of England from the 11th and 12th centuries onwards, yet it was on the banks of the Itchen and Test that dry fly fishing evolved, and in the middle to the late 1800s it was those gentleman of substance who had the time to spare who, unwittingly, created a form of sport which really appealed and that helped to shape the management of the river that we see today. It was those who had followed the teachings of those early dry fly fishing disciples Mottram,

Sheringham, Marryat and Halford and more lately, Lord Edward Gray, Skues, Dermot Wilson and Frank Sawyer who influenced the owners of this wonderful river. Dry fly fishing on the Itchen and Test became the way to fish and to increase this opportunity to practice the art, the landowners employed more and more river keepers to maintain, enhance or restore the rivers back to a state where they offered even more top quality dry fly fishing for wild brown trout.

Up and down the chalk streams of Hampshire, vast amounts of money were spent by these landowners on their particular beats, to such an extent that there arose great, but friendly, rivalry between beats and between rivers as to who could produce the best quality dry fly fishing. In those days access to the rivers was kept strictly to the owners and the owners' guests. It was only in the latter years that commercialism crept in and access has become more readily available, but skill constrained in most cases, according to the size of your bill roll! Fishing clubs have been formed, as have various fishing associations over the years, and each have acquired rights and tenancies as they have become available, again to such an extent that every inch of the bank of the River Itchen is owned and fished by somebody. Immoral as it may appear to some, if it was not for these landowners who loved their rivers and their sport and paid out of their own pockets for the rivers to be protected and improved and maintained properly for their own use, we would not have such fragile gems for people to enjoy today.

In 1907 the Test & Itchen Association was formed by the landowners who aimed to establish a common and agreed management strategy for both the River Itchen and Test. This Association works closely now with all the relevant government agencies and together the overall management of our rivers is in good, capable hands. Of course, there are many problems to face each year as any river and its catchment must do in the modern age, as towns and villages expand and the demands for water and space grow. I believe that each river must strive to have in place the main foundation stone of a fishery management philosophy.

Each river and its total catchment must be viewed in the context of one single aquatic ecosystem, which is a managed unit.

Proceeding onwards, as more and more people took up the art of dry fly fishing, demands for quality dry fly fishing grew; in some cases and on some beats, fishing pressure has been allowed to grow to such an extent that the self-sustaining stocks of brown trout were unable to supply the demand. Fisheries became overfished and before catch and release became popular, stocking with brown trout and imported rainbows became the recognized remedy in the early days. With this heavy stocking came the commensurate decline in the quality of the fishing experience and demand began to tail off. Fortunately, some of the forward-thinking owners and keepers had the foresight to establish fishery management policies that are now aimed at the protection and enhancement of the wild brown trout and its habitat with the aim to produce self-sustaining stocks of wild brown trout. By fighting hard to protect the river flows in quantity, by reducing abstraction, and quality, by more stringent pollution controls, further degradation is being controlled. By planning and lobbying for the establishment of a total catchment management plan that views the whole aquatic ecosystem in the context of one unit, further protection measures come into line, e.g., the control of detrimental land use practices, the encouragement of creating and enlarging buffer zones, and all the various uses of environmentally sustainable economic development principles.

CATCHMENT MANAGEMENT

Only by establishing this basic catchment management philosophy can any site-specific remedies really be contemplated with confidence. So many times in the past, time-consuming, labour intensive and expensive work has been undertaken attempting to remedy the symptoms of degradation in a fishery, when the causes of those symptoms are unclear or not understood or even unknown. For example, it is of limited benefit to regularly dredge silt from a stretch of river if the root cause of the build-up of silt is not identified. It will often be found that problems do not actually derive from within a river but rather beside the river or, in many cases, quite a distance from the river's edge.

Therefore, land uses practices and their effects within a catchment have to be studied in depth.

History teaches us that some river rehabilitation and management schemes have had limited success because they have been carried out as isolated projects without regard to the whole river catchment as an ecosystem, and we also find that the end result is often piecemeal rehabilitation, directed at the effects of the ecosystem disorder, rather than its causes, therefore, again, we have to manage our aquatic ecosystems as a whole, not in parts.

Important as this fundamental concept is, it is an ideal which is not always easily attainable. It is, at the same time, important to recognize that local rehabilitation works can often produce significant local benefits; for example, if excessive bankside grazing by livestock is a problem on a fishery, then treating the cause and the symptoms by fencing the river, are one and the same thing. On the other hand, it can be a waste of time constantly cleaning and restoring spawning gravels if the factor limiting survival is excessive silt laden water runoff.

Understanding the catchment is usually half the problem solved. Once the factors which affect the health of the aquatic ecosystem have been identified and understood, then site specific rehabilitation, restoration and conservation plans can be drawn up.

CHAPTER 53

PRACTICAL TECHNIQUES

With the history and philosophy lesson over, I would like to take you briefly through some more of the practical techniques used on the River Itchen. Bearing in mind all I have said.

Of course, it is all a matter of degree as to how any civil engineering is carried out, because the methods used on the placid, spring-fed rivers of the Hampshire Basin would not, for example, be man enough on the Yellowstone River here in Montana. The principles, however, are the same. Powerful spate rivers such as the Yellowstone will, and must, have their own tailor-made management techniques. On the spring-fed creeks of this continent (North America) chalk stream restoration and enhancement techniques would work once a program is formulated which takes into consideration local conditions. On the River Itchen, channel narrowing is undertaken where erosion has widened the channel to such an extent that the water is too shallow. By narrowing the channel, the flows are speeded up and this keeps the silt on the move, deepens the channel and improves macrophyte growth and, therefore, enhances good wild brown trout habitat. Care must be taken not to over narrow, as this can cause excessive erosion downstream especially if the 10/50/100-year historical flood events are not taken into consideration. Being a totally manmade river, the banks of the Itchen must be regularly repaired, as the river is always trying to return itself to its original natural state.

Lack of good natural spawning conditions have been shown to be a major constraint on the maintenance of the wild trout populations of the River Itchen. To address this problem, channel narrowing helps to keep spawning gravels clean and free from silt. Owing to the high calcium content of the water, gravels become naturally compacted over time, so regular raking and water jetting of these compacted substrates does open up more areas for potential spawning. At times, where gravels are not satisfactory, importation and planting of gravels of the right size is undertaken and has been proven successful. Predator control is an ongoing occupation for river keepers: mink, otters, herons, cormorants, pike and human poachers constantly must be addressed. Constant vigilance is the watchword. As I tell my students who aspire to become river keepers in England, to be successful in managing and keeping a wild trout fishery one has to be, firstly, fully conversant with the whole life cycle of the wild brown trout and all its needs for survival, from egg through to at least 4 years old, and then to be able to pinpoint and identity all the limiting factors that control survival of the trout throughout this cycle and be capable of treating these factors. To think like a wild brown trout may be an over simplification, but I find it is a good and simple maxim to follow.

CHAPTER 54

TOWARDS GOOD HABITAT MANAGEMENT

So, let's take the theme of this meeting, 'putting the native back into wild trout', by highlighting the fundamental principles of good and practical river management that will lead us towards achieving that goal.

Experience has taught me over the past 40 years of involvement with the chalk streams of England, that nature knows best and that in no way can we change her ways; we can, however, help and assist her in the healing process of degraded streams. By understanding how nature works, we may be able to create or recreate the right conditions for a species of fish that may never have inhabited that stream. Not until all the detrimental land use practices and storm water runoff processes within the catchment have been identified and, where necessary, mitigation and control measures implemented, will any major stream rehabilitation be effective or carried out with any confidence. So good catchment management is a priority.

Before any rehabilitation work on a stream is even contemplated, let alone planned, a historical assessment must be made of the stream and its catchment to ascertain what the pristine conditions were like and how and why conditions have changed through time down to the present. This assessment may reveal that it is not feasible or desirable to return the stream back to its pristine state. On the other hand, it may reveal that all the stream needs is added protection and nature will do the restoration.

This initial survey will, therefore, pinpoint and identify all the limiting factors that are controlling survival of the target species. Once this survey and assessment is completed and given water quantity, quality and that all seasonal flow fluctuations and temperatures are acceptable, we are now armed with sufficient information to plan and design the restoration works necessary to recreate or create the right conditions that allow for the establishment, restoration, or enhancement, of a self-sustaining stock of wild brown trout. The result may be, however, a stream that is quite different from its historical pristine state, yet what has been produced is now a functional stream whose stability is maintained by and is compatible with all the prevailing catchment conditions.

To help us towards achieving this goal there is a five-stage process which will underpin any rehabilitation program which determines the ultimate success of this program.

These stages are:
1. A historical catchment and stream assessment which includes identifying limiting factors.
2. Planning
3. Design
4. Construction
5. Evaluation

It cannot be overemphasized how essential it is that after completion of any rehabilitation program that the project has to be evaluated accurately and to ensure this the evaluation must be incorporated into the scheme of things at the planning stage. Unfortunately, in my neck of the woods, evaluation to date has ranged from a glance over a road bridge, to a tramp up the stream with a fishing rod, through to the occasional electro fishing check. I do question these types of evaluation methodology, because to be of any value the evaluation must be performed in a repeatable and standardized form i.e. regular assessments have to be made for a period of at least two complete life cycles of the target species – e.g. wild brown trout in a chalk stream would be 8 years. Without consistent standards of evaluation how can we adjust and learn from our mistakes and plough any new-found knowledge and experience into future projects?

Yes, I believe man can put the 'native' back into wild brown trout. Man has the knowledge and expertise – all that is needed is the will and to remember that any rehabilitation projects are approached in a well-ordered and standardized manner. With all the stream classifications now available and with the right data, methodologies, models, monitoring, evaluation, and case history studies, all these should be blended into a useful process whereby habitats can be assessed, improvements planned, effects and responses predicted, monitoring designed and performed, construction assessed, and post-project evaluation completed, all in a repeatable and standardized form. If anyone doubts that this is possible, let us just remember that man went to the moon and back safely, just because the late Jack Kennedy said that man would.

Ron Holloway RIP

23rd April 1936 – 25th November 2016

The river keeper's farewell to his river.

"A Farewell"

Flow down, cold rivulet to the sea,
Thy tribute wave deliver:
No more by thee my steps will be,
For ever and ever.

Flow, softly flow, by lawn and lea,
A rivulet then a river:
Nowhere by thee my steps will be,
For ever and ever.

But here will sign thine alder tree,
And here thine aspen shiver,
And here by thee will hum the bee,
For ever and ever.

A thousand suns will stream on thee,
A thousand moons will quiver,
But not by thee my steps will be,
For ever and ever.

Tennyson